Shakespeare-ience
Julius Caesar

Dr. Robert D. Strickland

Perfection Learning®

Editorial Director	Julie A. Schumacher
Editorial Research and Feature Writer	Wim Coleman
Design	Michelle Glass
Art Research	Lisa Lorimor
Cover Art	Michael Aspengren

© 2005 **Perfection Learning**®

Please visit our Web site at:
www.perfectionlearning.com

Reinforced Library Binding: ISBN: 978-0-7569-1761-6 or **3960502**

Paperback: ISBN 978-0-7891-6130-7 or **3960501**

6 7 8 BB 22 21 20

Printed in the United States of America

Table of Contents

Introductory Material

About This Program 6

Of Patricians and Plebeians 7

The Story of *Julius Caesar* 8

Working with Shakespeare's Language 10

Strategies for Reading Shakespeare. 13

Frequently Used Words 14

Preparing for Speaking Parts 16

How to Have a Shakespeare-ience 17

Choosing Your Persona 18

Understanding Improvisation 19

Caesar's Victorious Return to Rome 20

The Play

Act I 21

    Cast of Characters 22

    Scene i *or* Citizens Prefer Caesar 23

    Scene ii *or* A Dire Warning 29

    Scene iii *or* The Plot Thickens 46

    Reacting to Act I 56

Act II 57

    Scene i *or* Decisions, Decisions 58

    Scene ii *or* Dream Interpretations 76

    Scenes iii and iv *or* The Tension Grows 84

    Reacting to Act II 90

Act III 91
    Scene i *or* Murder and Mayhem 92
    Scenes ii and iii *or* Crowd Control 111
    Reacting to Act III 130

Act IV 131
    Scene i *or* Three-Way Split 132
    Scenes ii and iii *or* With Friends Like These, Who Needs Enemies? . . . 136
    Reacting to Act IV 158

Act V 159
    Scene i *or* Face to Face 160
    Scenes ii and iii *or* The Battle Begins 169
    Scenes iv and v *or* The Battle's Over 178
    Reacting to Act V 187

Reacting to the Play 188

Background Information

Life in Ancient Rome 190
Shakespeare's Life 194
Shakespeare's Times: The Question of Succession 196
Shakespeare's Theatre 197
Shakespeare's Sources: The Legend of Julius Caesar 200
Julius Caesar Timeline 201
Image Credits 203

Dr. Robert D. Strickland is Executive Director in the Division of Life Skills and Special Projects for all of the arts disciplines in the Miami-Dade County Public Schools. He received a BS in music education from the University of Tennessee, an MA and MFA in theatre from the University of Miami, and an Ed.D in Educational Leadership from Nova Southeastern University. He is a past president of the Florida Association for Theatre Education and a member of the Florida Department of Education writing team for the theatre teacher certification examination, theatre curriculum frameworks/ standards, and theatre course descriptions. He was a senior consultant for developing and writing a high school textbook that received the 1999 Distinguished Book Award from the American Alliance for Theatre Education.

Dr. Strickland has taught at the elementary, secondary, college, and university levels. He received the 1997 Administrator of the Year awards from both the Florida Association for Theatre Education and the Dade Association for Theatre Education. In 2000, Dr. Strickland was awarded the Herbert A. Drew, Jr., Memorial Award for Excellence in Education from Nova Southeastern University.

Dr. Strickland participated in the conceptualization of *Shakespeare-ience,* as well as the writing and editing of the program.

Wim Coleman, a freelance novelist and playwright, has frequently written about Shakespeare for students. Mr. Coleman holds an MA in teaching in both English and education from Drake University. Coleman has worked as an actor, director, set designer, and scene shop manager. He has taught, directed, and performed in numerous Shakespeare productions and has edited several Shakespeare plays in Perfection Learning's popular *Parallel Text* series. His most recent book for Perfection Learning is *Stages of History,* a collection of one-act plays based on American history.

Mr. Coleman wrote several background essays for *Julius Caesar* as well as the informational notes found at the bottom of most pages.

About This Program

This program was designed to help you discover the world of Shakespeare and in particular the story of Julius Caesar. Shakespeare's plays were meant to be seen and heard. In his day, rowdy audiences responded to them with applause, tears, and jeers. Playwrights were more interested in audiences than in readers, so students did not study the plays as they do today.

This book takes the fear out of studying Shakespeare and puts back the fun. Our approach to *Julius Caesar* is different in several important ways.

- First, you will create a character or persona that will live within the context of the play. You will participate every day, not just on the days you are reading the part of one of the characters with lines in the text.

- You will find that Shakespeare is not that difficult, contrary to what you might have heard. We have provided you with a

number of guiding features, such as on-page plot summaries, word and phrase definitions, and historical insights, to help you with the places that might be troublesome.

- By examining the thoughts of the characters through improvisation and then applying your understanding of the character's actions to the script, you will speak and hear the words of Shakespeare as he intended. You'll find that the words on these pages come to life when the art of theatre is used to study them.

Have fun with this program. While you probably won't mount a full production of *Julius Caesar*, you *will* learn to use hand and body gestures, expressive speech, and blocking (stage movements) as you read. If you trust yourself and jump into examining this world through the eyes of Shakespeare's characters and your own personas, you will truly have a Shakespeare-ience.

Of Patricians and Plebeians

Julius Caesar dramatizes the struggle to control Rome after Caesar's assassination. Both Shakespeare and his Elizabethan audience knew who finally won. They also had no trouble understanding references to Roman beliefs and customs. However, most people today need more historical background than Shakespeare provides.

Kings ruled Rome for many years. Rome's last king was the tyrant Tarquin, an evil man who abused his power.

The republic developed a government of many levels, each with its particular duties. Power was kept in the hands of the patricians—those from old noble families—and wealthy middle-class citizens. Working-class citizens—called plebeians—were represented in government but had little actual power. Slaves, foreigners, and women were not allowed to hold office or vote.

The highest-ranking officials in the Roman republic were two consuls, who presided over the Senate and all elections. Caesar first became a consul in 59 B.C.

The consuls selected the members of the Senate—Rome's ruling body. The Senate's decrees became law unless vetoed by the tribunes.

The ten tribunes were the only plebeians who were elected officials. In theory, the tribunes could check the power of the senators and protect the rights of ordinary citizens. They had the power to veto Senate decrees. Tribunes were also by law immune from arrest. This prevented the aristocrats from silencing a tribune by throwing him in jail. Consequently, many tribunes were assassinated when they stood in the way of a senator's ambition.

The republic was certainly not a democracy and was not without its problems. The patricians spent a lot of time fighting among themselves, each trying to get just a little more power. During times of crisis, a powerful man could become dictator.

Julius Caesar on his throne

member of lower social class

The Story of *Julius Caesar*

The play begins in ancient Rome during the feast of Lupercal. A group of plebeians (Roman commoners) has gathered to watch a parade honoring Julius Caesar's recent civil war victories. Two tribunes (representatives of the plebeians) scold them for supporting the ambitious, undemocratic Caesar; they send the plebeians away.

Julius Caesar arrives for the day's festivities. Vain, superstitious, aging, Caesar nevertheless has more than a trace of haughty grandeur about him. When a soothsayer warns him to beware the Ides (or middle) of March, Caesar disdainfully ignores him.

Then, during a public ceremony, Caesar's friend Mark Antony offers Caesar a crown three times. Each time, the crowd cheers wildly, hoping that Caesar will become king. But each time, Caesar reluctantly pushes the crown away. He finally goes home after suffering an attack of epilepsy.

Meanwhile, the politician Cassius has been warning another nobleman, Brutus, of Caesar's ambitions. If Caesar becomes king, asks Cassius, what will become of freedom-loving men like themselves? The idealistic Brutus loathes Caesar's ambition, but loves Caesar personally. So he is reluctant to join Cassius' conspiracy.

That night brings a storm filled with supernatural wonders. A wild lion roams the streets, men burst into flame, the dead rise from their graves, and blood rains onto the Capitol. Unafraid of such sights, the cunning Cassius throws several letters into Brutus' window. Written as if they were from different citizens, the letters urge Brutus to take action against Caesar.

Late that night, Cassius brings the conspirators to Brutus' house. Brutus agrees that Caesar must be killed the next day and takes charge of the conspiracy. The visitors leave, ready for tomorrow's assassination. Brutus' wife, Portia, senses impending danger and begs her husband to tell her of his plans. As proof of her loyalty to Brutus, Portia has wounded herself in the thigh. Moved by this gesture, Brutus promises to tell her the truth as soon as he can.

Caesar has spent a sleepless night worrying about the ominous storm. His wife, Calpurnia, has dreamed of seeing his statue spouting fountains of blood. She begs him not to go to the Capitol that morning to meet with the Roman Senate. Caesar reluctantly agrees to stay at home.

But the conspirator Decius quickly arrives to accompany Caesar to the Capitol. He insists that Calpurnia's dream is actually favorable, signifying that Caesar's blood is revitalizing to Rome. Also, Decius says that the senators have decided to crown Caesar that very day. If Caesar stays home, he'll miss his opportunity to become king. Caesar decides to go to the Capitol, after all.

Just outside the Capitol, Caesar again meets the soothsayer, who warns him that the Ides of March have not yet passed. Caesar's friend Artemidorus also approaches him with a letter revealing the conspirators' plot. But Caesar brusquely turns Artemidorus away, leaving the letter unread.

Inside the Capitol, senators implore Caesar to allow a banished nobleman to return to Rome. Caesar arrogantly refuses. As he boasts of his inflexibility, the conspirators attack, stabbing him again and again. The last knife thrust comes from Brutus; Caesar dies knowing that one of his dearest friends has betrayed him.

While Caesar's supporters flee the Capitol in fear, the conspirators ceremoniously bathe their hands in Caesar's blood. Mark Antony arrives and views the scene with horror. Nevertheless, he promises to hear the conspirators' reasons for their deed. Against the wishes of Cassius, Brutus agrees to let Antony speak at Caesar's funeral.

At the funeral, Brutus gives the first oration. He carefully explains to the crowd that Caesar was killed solely because he was a threat to Roman liberty. The people are swayed by Brutus' speech and proclaim him a hero. Overly confident, Brutus leaves the funeral before Antony's oration.

As he begins to speak, Antony cunningly claims to have no intention of praising Caesar. But little by little, he sways the crowd against the conspirators. At last, feigning reluctance, he reads Caesar's will to the crowd. When the people learn that Caesar left money and lands to them, they go on a murderous rampage. They even lynch the innocent poet Cinna because he has the same name as one of the conspirators.

Cassius and Brutus flee the city. Caesar's grandnephew Octavius, the statesman Lepidus, and Mark Antony jointly take command of Rome.

While preparing for war near Sardis in Asia Minor, Brutus accuses Cassius of accepting bribes, and the two men bitterly quarrel. They quickly reconcile, and Brutus admits that his ill temper has been caused by news of Portia's suicide back in Rome. Cassius marvels at Brutus' stoical forbearance in the face of such grief. Over Cassius' objections,

Brutus insists on attacking the forces of Antony and Octavius at Philippi. That night, Brutus is awakened by the appearance of Caesar's ghost, who tells Brutus that he will see him again at Philippi.

Before parting for battle the next morning, Cassius and Brutus bid one another an emotional farewell, realizing that they may never meet again. They promise to kill themselves rather than face the humiliation of defeat.

During the fighting, Cassius sends his friend Titinius to observe some nearby troops. Cassius' slave Pindarus watches Titinius, whom he sees surrounded by mounted soldiers; Pindarus mistakenly believes Titinius to be taken prisoner. Convinced of his own defeat, the despairing Cassius offers Pindarus his freedom if he will kill him. Pindarus slays Cassius and flees.

But Titinius has been surrounded by friendly soldiers, not enemies, and he returns to Cassius' tent with news of Brutus' victory in battle. Finding Cassius dead, Titinius kills himself. When Brutus discovers the bodies of Cassius and Titinius, he senses the presence of Caesar's avenging spirit.

Brutus' troops are soon defeated in further fighting, and Brutus contemplates suicide. He begs three of his followers to slay him; Clitus and Dardanus refuse, but Strato agrees to hold the sword while Brutus falls upon it. Brutus does so, speaking Caesar's name as he dies.

Antony and Octavius arrive and find Brutus' body. Antony praises Brutus as "the noblest Roman of them all," for he was the only conspirator who acted out of righteous motives. Octavius agrees, ordering that Brutus be buried with full honors.

Brutus's wife kills herself

Working with Shakespeare's Language

When you first begin reading Shakespeare, you may find his language intimidating and confusing. You will discover, however, that the more Shakespeare you read and the more you know about his writing, the easier it becomes.

Keep in mind that language is a living thing, constantly growing and changing. New words are invented and new definitions for old words are added. Since Shakespeare wrote more than 400 years ago, it is not surprising that his work seems challenging to today's readers. To help you with the meaning of the text, unfamiliar words and phrases have been defined for you in the side margins of this book. You may also find a dictionary helpful for this purpose. Beyond the meaning of the words, however, there are stylistic devices that can help you understand Shakespeare.

Blank Verse and Iambic Pentameter

Like most dramatists of his time, Shakespeare frequently used blank verse in his plays. In **blank verse**, the text is written in measured lines that do not rhyme. Look at the following example.

> Let's carve him as a dish fit for the gods,
> Not hew him as a carcass fit for hounds.
> And let our hearts, as subtle masters do,
> Stir up their servants to an act of rage…

$$\text{Let's } \overset{\cup}{} \text{CARVE} \overset{/}{} \mid \text{him } \overset{\cup}{} \text{AS} \overset{/}{} \mid \text{a } \overset{\cup}{} \text{DISH} \overset{/}{} \mid \text{fit } \overset{\cup}{} \text{FOR} \overset{/}{} \mid \text{the } \overset{\cup}{} \text{GODS} \overset{/}{}$$

$$\text{Not } \overset{\cup}{} \text{HEW} \overset{/}{} \mid \text{him } \overset{\cup}{} \text{AS} \overset{/}{} \mid \text{a } \overset{\cup}{} \text{CAR} \overset{/}{} \mid \text{cass } \overset{\cup}{} \text{FIT} \overset{/}{} \mid \text{for } \overset{\cup}{} \text{HOUNDS} \overset{/}{}$$

The length of a line of verse is measured by counting the stresses. This length is known as the **meter**, and when there are five stresses, as in the preceding lines, the pattern is known as **pentameter**. When the rhythm follows an unstressed/stressed pattern, it is called **iambic**. Much of Shakespeare's work is written in **iambic pentameter**.

Of course, Shakespeare was not rigid about this format. He sometimes varied the lines by putting accents in unusual places, by having lines with more or fewer than ten syllables, and by varying where pauses occur. An actor's interpretation can also add variety. (Only a terrible actor would deliver lines in a way that makes the rhythm sound obvious or repetitious!)

Prose

In addition to verse, Shakespeare wrote speeches in **prose**, or language without rhythmic structure. Look at Antony's second speech on page 124 ("Why friends, you go to do you know not what.") where Antony speaks to the Plebeians. Try beating out the rhythm of Antony's speech, and you will find that it usually follows the pattern of iambic pentameter. But if you try to impose the same rhythm on the Plebeians' speeches that follow, you'll discover that it doesn't work at all.

Shakespeare often uses prose for comic speeches, to show madness, and for characters of lower social rank such as servants. His upper-class characters generally do not speak in prose. But these weren't hard-and-fast rules as far as Shakespeare was concerned. Many of his servants speak in verse, and some of his noble characters (Hamlet, for example) occasionally speak in prose.

Imagery

Imagery refers to vibrant, colorful language that allows readers or listeners to picture things in their mind's eye and to make an emotional connection with the writing. This highly descriptive language appeals to one or more of the five senses— touch, taste, hearing, smell, and sight. How many sensory images can you find in the following speech?

And Caesar's spirit, ranging for revenge,
With Até by his side come hot from hell,
Shall in these confines with a monarch's
voice

Cry "Havoc!" and let slip the dogs of war,
That this foul deed shall smell above
the earth
With carrion men, groaning for burial.

In addition to sensory words, images are often conveyed through the use of **figures of speech** such as simile, metaphor, or personification.

A **simile** is a comparison between two things that uses the words *like* or *as*. Look at the following examples.

Why, man, he doth bestride the narrow world
Like a Colossus, and we petty men
Walk under his huge legs and peep about . . .

You show'd your teeth like apes and fawn'd
like hounds
And bow'd like bondmen, kissing Caesar's
feet,
Whilst damnèd Casca, like a cur, behind
Struck Caesar on the neck.

In the first quote, Caesar is compared to Colossus, a 100-foot-tall statue. In the second, Antony compares Brutus and the other conspirators to apes, slaves, and dogs.

A **metaphor** is also a comparison between two unlike things, but the words *like* and *as* are left out. In the following passage, Caesar is compared to a high-flying bird.

These growing feathers pluck'd from
Caesar's wing
Will make him fly an ordinary pitch,
Who else would soar above the view of men
And keep us all in servile fearfulness.

Another type of imagery used extensively by Shakespeare is **personification**, giving human qualities to inanimate objects or ideas. In the following lines, the river Tiber is personified as a frightened woman.

Have you not made an universal shout,
That Tiber trembled underneath her banks
To hear the replication of your sounds
Made in her concave shores?

Contractions

As you know, contractions are words that have been combined by substituting an apostrophe for a letter or letters that have been removed. Contractions were as common in Shakespeare's time as they are today. For example, we use *it's* as a contraction for the words *it is*. In Shakespeare's writing you will discover that *'tis* means the same thing. Many other examples can be found in the list of Frequently Used Words on pages 14-15.

Shakespeare often used the apostrophe to shorten words so that they would fit into the rhythm pattern of a line. This is especially true of verbs ending in *-ed*. Note that in Shakespeare's plays, the *-ed* at the end of a verb is pronounced as a separate syllable. Therefore, *walked* would be pronounced as two syllables, *walk•ed*, while *walk'd* would be only one. We have added accent marks (walkèd) to help you remember to pronounce *-ed* aloud.

You will learn about other elements of Shakespeare's language such as **puns** and **irony** as they occur in the text.

Finally, if you can't figure out every word in the play, don't get discouraged. The people in Shakespeare's audience couldn't either. At that time, language was changing rapidly and standardized spelling, punctuation, grammar, and even dictionaries did not exist. Besides, Shakespeare loved to play with words. He made up new combinations, like *fat-guts* and *mumble-news*. He often changed one part of speech for another, as in "cursing claims and deep *exclaims*." To make matters worse, the actors probably spoke at a rate of 140 words per minute. But the audience didn't strain to catch every word. They went to a Shakespeare play for the same reasons we go to a movie—to get caught up in the story and the acting, to have a great laugh, an exciting adventure, or a good cry.

Strategies for Reading Shakespeare

You will find many features in this book designed to help you understand Shakespeare's language. In addition, there are some basic reading strategies that active readers use for all types of text. As you prepare to read *Julius Caesar*, you may find the following strategic plan useful.

Preview. First, to get a general idea of the events in the play, "read the edges" of the text. Read the summaries at the top of each page. Then skim the definitions and questions in the side margins and examine any images that appear. This will give you a general idea of what the text is about before you actually begin to read it.

Visualize. Try to put yourself into the world of the play by picturing the setting in your mind's eye. Envision how the characters might look and sound as they move within their surroundings. Studying images and reading through the setting and stage directions will help to fire up your imagination.

Read. Read a page using the side notes to help with difficult words and phrases. Go back and reread the page a second time or as many times as necessary until you can understand the text without using the side notes. This may be more difficult in the beginning and take more time than reading

modern writing, but don't be discouraged. Most students find that comprehension becomes easier and easier as the play goes on.

Connect. Active readers often make connections with the text. An event in their reading might remind them of something that happened to them or a friend, or they might see similarities between the text and a movie, book, or TV show they have seen. Also, because Shakespeare is quoted so frequently, readers are likely to come across familiar phrases and sayings.

Evaluate. As you read, evaluate the characters' words and actions and form opinions about them. Do you approve or disapprove of how they act? What are their motives? What are their strengths and weaknesses? Do certain actions make you change your mind about a character?

Enrich. Surround your study of *Julius Caesar* with humor and high-interest material. The notes at the bottom of most pages and the essays in the front and back of the book provide background information. The "Tales from the Stage" feature contains colorful theatrical anecdotes. The suggestions for props and in-class staging will also help to immerse you in Shakespeare's world.

Frequently Used Words

The following words and phrases are found frequently in Shakespeare's plays. The more of them you know, the easier your reading will be.

afore . . . . . . before

alack . . . . expression of sorrow or regret

alas . . . . expression of unhappiness, pity, or concern

anon . . . . at once, immediately

an't . . . . if it

art . . . . are

ay, aye . . . . . . yes

bawdy . . . . . . indecent

beseech . . . . . beg

betimes . . . . . at times, occasionally

bid . . . . ask

by my troth . . . truly

coz . . . . cousin; relative

dost . . . . you do (second person singular of the verb "do")

doth . . . . he, she, it does (third person singular of the verb "do")

e'en . . . . even

e'er . . . . ever

enow . . . . . . enough

ere . . . . before

exeunt . . . . . theatre term meaning "everyone leaves the stage"

fain . . . . willingly

fay . . . . faith

fie . . . . O

foresworn . . . . denied

hadst . . . . you had (second person singular past tense of the verb "have")

hap . . . . perhaps

hark you . . . . listen

hast, hath . . . . you have; he, she, it has (second and third person singular of "have")

hence . . . . . . away from this place

hie . . . . hurry

humor . . . . . . mood

humour . . . . . liquid

is't . . . . is it

knave . . . . . . rascal

14

late . . . . . . recently

marry . . . . . I swear
mine . . . . . . my

nay . . . . no
ne'er . . . . . . never

o'er . . . . over
oft . . . . often

perchance . . . perhaps
pray . . . . invite

rest you merry . have a good day

saucy . . . . . . rude
scurvy . . . . . disgusting
shalt . . . . . . you shall (second person singular of "shall")
shrift . . . . . . confession of sins
sirrah . . . . . . sir (a form of address implying inferiority)
soft . . . . wait
spake . . . . . . said
stay . . . . stop
straight . . . . . at once

sup . . . . to eat (often the evening meal)

thee, thou . . . . you
thence . . . . . . from that time (or place) on
thine . . . . yours
thither . . . . . . there; to that place
thrice . . . . . . three times
thy . . . . your
'tis . . . . it is
tut, tush . . . . . mild expression of disapproval
'twixt . . . . . . between

wast, wert . . . . were
whence . . . . . where (from what place)
wherefore . . . why
whither . . . . . where (to what place)
wilt . . . . will, must
writ . . . . written

ye . . . . you
yea . . . . yes
yon, yond . . . . that

Preparing for Speaking Parts

At least once during your study of *Julius Caesar*, you will be assigned a speaking part to perform for an upcoming class. In order to feel comfortable in this role and to respect the efforts of other students reading with you, you will need to prepare beforehand. If you are unsure about how to do this, try using the following plan.

Comprehend. Make sure you understand the meaning of what your character says. If you are unsure, use the strategies on page 13.

Analyze. Determine your character's attitude during the scene. What is the character's mood? Does this mood change during the scene? Are the character's thoughts and words the same? Or does the character say one thing and mean another? What is your character's motivation? What does the character want? What is the attitude toward other characters in the scene? Is there a conflict? What is it?

Plan. Decide how you will use your body and voice to create your character. What gestures will you use? Where and when will you move? How will you use your voice? Changes in the tempo (fast, slow); pitch (high, low); and quality (nasal, raspy, etc.) of your voice can help the audience understand your character. If needed, you can put sticky notes in your text to remind you of where you want to change your voice or move.

Practice. You probably won't have a chance to rehearse with others in your scene, but you should still practice your own part. Ask a friend or family member to read lines with you and/or videotape you. You can also practice reading your part into a tape recorder.

Warm Up. Here are a few exercises to make your voice and body more flexible and responsive.

- Stand tall and inhale on a count of four; hold your breath for a count of four; and then exhale on a count of eight. Make sure that your shoulders are relaxed and do not rise up as you breathe. Your lower stomach area should be slowly moving out as you inhale, and in as you exhale.
- Next, repeat the same exercise and while you are exhaling, hum the letter M. You will feel a tingle in your face from the vibration of the sound. After you have done this several times, try a few tongue twisters. Here is one to start with:

  > Amidst the mists and coldest frosts,
  > With stoutest wrists and loudest boasts,
  > He thrusts his fists against the post
  > And still insists he sees the ghosts.

- Stand tall with your feet shoulder-width apart. Bend over slowly and reach for or touch the floor. Relax and breathe. Bend your knees more and then straighten your legs slowly. Slowly round up your body to a standing position. Repeat the whole exercise twice.

Act and React. As you present your scene, remember to face the audience and speak loudly enough to be heard throughout the room. Holding your book and your head up as you read will help your voice project out to the audience. Finally, listen, really listen, to what the other characters are saying so that you can respond realistically and pick up cues promptly.

How to Have a Shakespeare-ience

There is an old saying that to really understand someone you need to walk a mile in his or her shoes. This study of *Julius Caesar* borrows from that old adage by asking you to study the play by becoming a Roman citizen living in 44 B.C. You will "walk" for many days in that person's "shoes."

By seeing the Roman world at this time through eyes other than your own, you will gain a new perspective and interact with other characters that shape that world. The characters that you create will not actually speak within the text of the play, but all are affected by the circumstances and actions of the speaking characters. So you may not be Caesar, but you may be his attendant or one of his spies. You may not be Brutus, but you may be a cook in his home or one of his wife's servants.

Each of you will be part of the action of the play, and from time to time will be called upon to be one of the traditional speaking characters as well. In addition, you will be creating events and situations that are only implied by the action of the play. For example, the victorious Caesar enters Rome on the Lupercal holiday. If you were a servant to Caesar, what would your duties be in preparing for the festivities? How would you celebrate? And, as the story of the play unfolds, how do the various events that take place affect you and your world?

You will be discovering what life was like in Rome hundreds of years ago. The creation of your character, or **persona**, as we will call it throughout the rest of the book, will be based on elements in the text, historical information, human nature, and your imagination. You will discover the events that influenced the lives of the people in Caesar's Rome and ultimately played important roles in the unfolding of this story. By being immersed this way into the story and the play, you will be experiencing *Julius Caesar* as if you were there. This is what we mean by having a **Shakespeare–ience**.

Choosing Your Persona

As you can see in the following list, there were many kinds of people that made up the population of ancient Rome. Your teacher will either assign one of these personas to you or ask you to choose one from the list. In either case, you will begin with only a name or occupation. It will be your job to develop your persona and turn him or her into a complete character. All characters will be from the plebeian or lower levels of Roman society—the common people. You will start developing your persona by responding to items on a personality profile. As the play progresses, you will find questions and directions, labeled **Persona Journal** and **Persona Action**, which will guide you. Remember that you are always to respond and react as your persona would.

Your stay in the world of *Julius Caesar* will be ruled by the following assumptions. 1) Assume that almost all characters listed below can be either male or female. Therefore, it is not necessary to limit persona choices to traditional gender roles. 2) Assume that all personas travel to the battlefields in Acts IV and V. 3) To avoid crowding the acting area, some Persona Action directions will call for **representatives** from your group. Either in a group meeting, or as your teacher directs, decide how representatives can be chosen so that everyone has equal time on stage. 4) Some directions will call for "in place" reactions, which mean that you will react in place.

Citizens of Ancient Rome

Cook	Ink Maker	Iron/Lead Worker	Soap Maker	Landowner
Guard	Wine Maker	Wood Carver	Fishmonger	Grain Dealer
Watchman	Stable Keeper	Candle Maker	Fisherman	Armor Maker
Attendant	Potter	Slave	Cabinet Maker	Cooper (Barrel Maker)
Messenger	Farmer	Carpenter	Merchant	Butcher
Secretary	Ox-goad	Blacksmith	Dye Worker	Porter
Copyist	Mule Train Driver	Beekeeper	Sculptor	Estate Manager
Maid	Tailor	Shepherd	Oar & Boat Maker	Ploughman
Physician	Furrier	Hunter	Craftsperson	Reaper
Seamstress	Cobbler	Tax Collector	Baker	Architect
Laundress	Tanner	Rent Collector	Soothsayer	Hairdresser
Weaver	Mill Worker	Jeweler	Soldier	Gladiator
Embroiderer	Ale/Mead Maker	Goldsmith	Bath Attendant	Librarian
Musician	Roofer	Scribe	Toga Maker	Tutor
Artist	Stone Mason		Clerk	

Understanding Improvisation

It is possible that you have heard the word **improvisation** in connection to theatre, music, stand-up comedy, or dance. Improvisation may sometimes be referred to as role-playing. In this study of *Julius Caesar*, improvisation exercises before each scene will be used as a discovery tool to explore the characters and the events in the play.

Literally, to improvise is to speak or act out a situation without a script or preconceived way of presenting the scene. You are given the framework of the situation such as the conflict and the characters, and without advanced planning, you make up the scene's dialogue spontaneously. You must find a way to resolve conflicts and overcome obstacles in order to accomplish the objectives of the characters. Direct your concentration toward the situation and the other participants while keeping an open mind about what your character is experiencing. In addition, be receptive to any new information introduced by your partner(s). React honestly.

Improvisation trains people to think on different levels. It helps develop imagination, concentration, self-esteem, self-confidence, observation skills, listening skills, problem-solving skills, and thinking skills.

The following exercises will introduce you to the process of improvisation.

Partner Activities

- A fortune-teller says that you are going to achieve great things; try to get him/her to tell you more.
- You think your husband/boyfriend could be more of an achiever by breaking some rules; try to convince him of this.
- Try to persuade someone you know that it's in his/her best interests to betray a mutual acquaintance.

- You've committed a crime, and a police detective seems to suspect you; try to convince him/her of your innocence.
- You're a wartime general. Someone wants to join your army, but you think he/she might be a spy for the other side; test his/her loyalty.

Group Activities

- With a group of seven to ten students, improvise waiting in an express checkout line (only ten items) at a grocery store. One customer has more than ten items, and his/her friend keeps bringing more items as you wait. This is the checkout person's first day after completing training.
- With a group of ten to fifteen students, improvise a situation where a local radio station is doing a remote location set-up, and as a promotion is giving away tickets to an upcoming concert. There are only three pairs of tickets to give away, and more than ten people show up to win them. Each person must convince the DJ to give him/her the tickets.

Julius Caesar Warm-Ups

- Caesar tells a group of friends that his wife Calpurnia seems unable to bear children. She reacts to Caesar's comment; their friends respond as well.
- Caesar explains to Antony why he distrusts Cassius.
- Portia complains to Brutus that he has been distant and irritable. She wants to know what's bothering him.
- Several plebeians and citizens hear the news that Caesar has been murdered.
- Brutus tells Cassius that he has seen Caesar's ghost.

Caesar's Victorious Return to Rome

Just as Shakespeare took liberties with historical facts to write *Julius Caesar*, the following improvisation takes historical liberties to establish an environment for this exercise. These conditions will allow you to experience, as a group, certain aspects of life in Rome during the time period of the play. Before the exercise, your teacher will divide you into two groups—**Caesarians**, those loyal to Caesar, and **Pompeians**, those who side with Pompey.

In the beginning of the first century B.C., Julius Caesar, Pompey, and Crassus joined together to rule Rome and its territories. This form of government was called a triumvirate, from the Latin *tres vir,* which means "three men." In 53 B.C., Crassus was killed in a battle against the Parthians. As a result, civil war broke out because Pompey and Caesar were not able to share power. In 48 B.C., Caesar defeated Pompey and soon after, Pompey's two sons as well. The play opens during Caesar's victorious return to Rome.

Before this activity begins, you will need to make a two-sided badge that can be pinned to your clothing. You will wear your badge throughout the play. One side of the badge will show that you side with Caesar and his followers, Antony, Lepidus, and Octavius. The other side will display your loyalty to Pompey and his followers: Brutus, Cassius, Casca, and the other conspirators. (The Cast of Characters on page 22 shows the affiliation of each character.) You will begin the play in the group indicated by your teacher. Members of each group will sit on opposite sides of the class in **Forums** (meeting places). However, and this is important, as the play progresses, you will encounter **Loyalty Checks**. At such times, you can switch sides by turning over your badge. If it is not too disruptive, your teacher may have you move to the other Forum as well.

This improvisational activity revolves around Caesar's return. Both groups are gathered in the Roman Forum awaiting Caesar's entrance with his entourage.

During the activity, you will hear announcements made from a central, raised speaker's platform. After you hear an announcement, improvise a reaction to it, and enter into conversation with other personas. Remember that you must respond to the news "in persona."

When the activity ends, answer the following questions in your Persona Journal.

- How did you react to the news from the four announcements?
- How do these announcements impact you and your group?
- Were you surprised by the reactions of others in your group? In the other group?

Julius Caesar ACT I

Louis Calhern as Caesar in the 1953 film directed by Joseph L. Mankiewicz

"I do fear the people choose Caesar for their king."

Cast of Characters

JULIUS CAESAR
MARK ANTONY
OCTAVIUS CAESAR
LEPIDUS
} The triumvirate that ruled after Caesar's death

CICERO
PUBLIUS
POPILIUS LENA
} Roman Senators

BRUTUS
CASSIUS
CASCA
TREBONIUS
CAIUS LIGARIUS
DECIUS BRUTUS
METELLUS CIMBER
CINNA
} Conspirators Against Caesar

FLAVIUS
MARULLUS
} Tribunes of the People

ARTEMIDORUS, a teacher

SOOTHSAYER, a fortune-teller

CINNA THE POET
ANOTHER POET

LUCILIUS
TITINIUS
MESSALA
YOUNG CATO
VOLUMNIUS
} Friends of Brutus and Cassius

VARRO
CLITUS
CLAUDIUS
STRATO
LUCIUS
DARDANIUS
} Officers or Servants to Brutus

PINDARUS, servant to Cassius

CALPURNIA, wife of Caesar

PORTIA, wife of Brutus

THE GHOST OF CAESAR

SENATORS, GUARDS, SERVANTS, ATTENDANTS, and OTHERS

TIME 44 B.C.

PLACES Rome, the camp near Sardis, the plains of Phillipi

Setting the Scene

JULIUS CAESAR

Act I, Scene i *or* Citizens Prefer Caesar

Critical Query: What conflict is introduced in this scene?

Time Capsule: Tribute

"What conquest brings he home?/What tributaries follow him to Rome..." is asked about Caesar in the scene that follows.

In Roman times, conquering armies were expected to return home with slaves, gold, and other treasure taken from the losing forces. A portion of these spoils of war belonged to the soldiers, while the balance funded public works such as baths, temples, aqueducts, theatres, and so forth.

Classroom Set Design

Move desks back to allow space for a playing area. The classroom should be divided into two forums (meeting places), one for the Caesarians and the other for Pompeians. A "street" separates the forums. The two groups may wish to decorate the walls of their forums or create banners that identify each side.

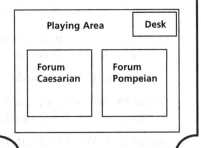

Behind the Scene: Tragedy

A **tragedy** is a serious work of literature that narrates the events leading to the downfall of a **tragic hero**, who is usually of noble birth and in almost every way displays noble qualities. His downfall is a result of a **tragic flaw** or fatal character weakness. As the play progresses, consider whether Brutus or Julius Caesar fits this definition and what each character's fatal flaw might be.

Warm-Up Improv

Your school has won the state championship. The main street of your town has been decorated with the school colors in anticipation of a celebration parade. Students from the losing school have destroyed some of the decorations. You and two friends, all members of the celebration committee, hear about the vandalism and discuss what is to be done.

Word Play: Are We Having Puns Yet?

A **pun** is a humorous play on words such as the title above, where the expected word "fun" is replaced by the word "puns." The most common variety of pun makes use of words with multiple meanings (fume, grate, case) or words with different spellings that sound alike (heart/hart, soul/sole, pair/pare). Be on the lookout for puns in the upcoming scene.

The play opens on a street in Rome where two tribunes, Flavius and Marullus, confront a group of ordinary citizens and scold them for being out on the streets on a workday and for not wearing work clothes that would identify their occupation. When asked about their work, the Cobbler responds with riddles and puns.

ACT I

Scene i. Rome. A Street

✳ [*Enter* FLAVIUS, MARULLUS, *and certain* COMMONERS *over the stage.*]

FLAVIUS. Hence! Home, you idle creatures, get you home!
　Is this a holiday? What, know you not,
　Being mechanical, you ought not walk
　Upon a labouring day without the sign
　Of your profession? Speak, what trade art thou?　　　5

CARPENTER. Why, sir, a carpenter.

MARULLUS. Where is thy leather apron and thy rule?
　What dost thou with thy best apparel on?
　You, sir, what trade are you?

COBBLER. Truly, sir, in respect of a fine workman, I am but, as　　10
　you would say, a cobbler.

MARULLUS. But what trade art thou? Answer me directly.

COBBLER. A trade, sir, that I hope I may use with a safe con-
　science, which is indeed, sir, a mender of bad soles.

MARULLUS. What trade, thou knave? Thou naughty knave,　　15
　what trade?

COBBLER. Nay, I beseech you, sir, be not out with me. Yet if
　you be out, sir, I can mend you.

PERSONA JOURNAL

A victorious Caesar returns today to Rome. How are you participating in the festivities?

over the stage: cross from one side of the stage to the other side

PERSONA ACTION

Representatives from the Caesarians are on stage when the tribunes enter. They listen and react to the events on the stage.

1 Hence: Go away

3 mechanical: manual laborers

4–5 the sign/Of your profession: your work clothes and tools

7 rule: ruler

10 in respect of: compared with

11 cobbler: shoemaker and also one who bungles his or her work

14 soles: used here as a pun, both as the bottom of shoes and the souls of people

15 naughty knave: worthless, wicked rascal

17 be not out: don't be angry

18 out: worn out shoes

✳ **Tribunes** Flavius and Marullus are tribunes—officials elected to represent the common people, or plebeians. Some critics have considered it odd that Flavius and Marullus are so scornful toward the very people they represent. But the tribunes are angry because the plebeians are enchanted with Caesar—a man who apparently wants to get rid of representative government and be their king.

The Cobbler continues to annoy the tribunes with his puns but finally explains that he and his friends are taking a holiday in order to see Caesar and to celebrate his victory over Pompey.

MARULLUS. What mean'st thou by that? Mend me, thou saucy
    fellow?   20

COBBLER. Why, sir, cobble you.

FLAVIUS. Thou art a cobbler, art thou?

COBBLER. Truly, sir, all that I live by is with the awl. I meddle
    with no tradesman's matters nor women's matters, but
    withal I am indeed, sir, a surgeon to old shoes: when they   25
    are in great danger, I recover them. As proper men as
    ever trod upon neat's leather have gone upon my
    handiwork.

FLAVIUS. But wherefore art not in thy shop today?
    Why dost thou lead these men about the streets?   30

COBBLER. Truly, sir, to wear out their shoes, to get myself into
    more work. But indeed, sir, we make holiday to see Caesar
    and to rejoice in his triumph.

? What three words could you use to describe the Carpenter? How would he speak his lines to the tribunes?

19 saucy: insolent

? Knowing that tribunes are powerful men, how would you speak the lines of the commoners (Carpenter, Cobbler) as they respond to the tribunes' questions with a bit of wordplay?

21 cobble you: fix your shoes

23 awl: a tool used to make holes in leather

25 withal: nevertheless

26 recover: repair or save; **proper:** respectable

27 neat's leather: cowhide

Oliver Ford Davies (dark uniform) plays Marullus as he confronts the commoners.
Royal Shakespeare Company, 1983.

Marullus becomes angry about the commoners' lack of loyalty and reminds them that they recently celebrated in the same way over Pompey's victories.

MARULLUS. Wherefore rejoice? What conquest brings he home?
What tributaries follow him to Rome   35
To grace in captive bonds his chariot wheels?
You blocks, you stones, you worse than senseless things!
O you hard hearts, you cruel men of Rome,
Knew you not Pompey? Many a time and oft
Have you climb'd up to walls and battlements,   40
To towers and windows, yea, to chimney tops,
Your infants in your arms, and there have sat
The livelong day, with patient expectation,
To see great Pompey pass the streets of Rome.

34 Wherefore: Why

35 tributaries: people who pay tributes of money to a conqueror

36 To grace in captive bonds: To decorate in chains

39 Pompey: co-ruler who was defeated by Caesar; **oft:** often

PERSONA JOURNAL

Were you a supporter of Pompey? Describe what you remember about Pompey's celebrations as referred to by Marullus.

TALES FROM THE STAGE
A Barrel of Laughs

Laurence Olivier (1907–1989) is regarded as one of the greatest Shakespearean actors of the 20th century. But some of his earliest performances were not exactly distinguished. For instance, he once played the small part of the tribune Flavius in an extremely low budget production of *Julius Caesar*. The actor playing Marullus had to stand on a small beer barrel while delivering his "Wherefore rejoice?" speech.

Marullus was wearing a pair of pants underneath his toga. The pants unfortunately fell down when he exclaimed, "Knew you not Pompey?" The pants gathered around his ankles and draped over the barrel so that poor Marullus couldn't move. Olivier laughed so hard that he had to leave the stage. He was fired the next morning.

Marullus continues to fume over the fickleness of the citizens and orders them to return home to pray for forgiveness for their ingratitude. After they leave, Flavius and Marullus decide to take different paths on their way to the Capitol, stripping any statues that might be decorated in Caesar's honor.

And when you saw his chariot but appear,   45
❋ Have you not made an universal shout,
That Tiber trembled underneath her banks
To hear the replication of your sounds
Made in her concave shores?
And do you now put on your best attire?   50
And do you now cull out a holiday?
And do you now strew flowers in his way
That comes in triumph over Pompey's blood?
Be gone!
Run to your houses, fall upon your knees,   55
Pray to the gods to intermit the plague
That needs must light on this ingratitude.

FLAVIUS. Go, go, good countrymen, and for this fault
Assemble all the poor men of your sort,
Draw them to Tiber banks, and weep your tears   60
Into the channel, till the lowest stream
Do kiss the most exalted shores of all.

[Exeunt all the COMMONERS.]

See whe'er their basest mettle be not mov'd;
They vanish tongue-tied in their guiltiness.
Go you down that way towards the Capitol;   65
This way will I. Disrobe the images
If you do find them deck'd with ceremonies.

47 Tiber: a river that runs through Rome

48 replication: echo

49 concave shores: overhanging banks

51 cull out: pick out

56 intermit: prevent

59 sort: rank

62 most exalted: highest

❓ Why are the tribunes angry with the commoners?

PERSONA ACTION

The Caesarians return to their Forum.

63 whe'er their … mov'd: if their worthless character hasn't been changed by what I've said

66 images: statues

67 deck'd with ceremonies: decorated with wreaths or garlands

❋ **A Global Event** *Julius Caesar* was probably first performed in 1599 at the brand-new Globe Theatre, on the south bank of the River Thames. In fact, *Julius Caesar* may have been the first drama ever performed in this famous theatre, where many more of Shakespeare's works would first appear. Perhaps Marullus is making a sly reference to the new theatre when he speaks of people making a "universal shout" that echoes across a river. The audience's cheering and applause may have been heard on the opposite bank of the Thames.

Flavius expresses his concern over the crowds of commoners out on the streets and vows to disburse any groups he finds. He is afraid that if Caesar sees such gatherings it could encourage him to seek even more power. The tribunes want to do everything they can to diminish Caesar's growing popularity.

MARULLUS. May we do so?
* You know it is the feast of Lupercal.

FLAVIUS. It is no matter. Let no images
    Be hung with Caesar's trophies. I'll about
    And drive away the vulgar from the streets;
    So do you too, where you perceive them thick.
    These growing feathers pluck'd from Caesar's wing
    Will make him fly an ordinary pitch,
    Who else would soar above the view of men
    And keep us all in servile fearfulness.

[Exeunt.]

70

75

Handwritten note (left margin): Ceaser needs to be humbeld

Handwritten note (right): They are afraid that Ceaser's going to be too powerful.

71 about: go around

72 vulgar: ordinary citizens

73 thick: gathered together

75 an ordinary pitch: at a lower height

? Explain the bird metaphor in lines 74–77.

? Why do you think Flavius is concerned about Caesar?

76 else: otherwise

77 in servile fearfulness: in fear as slaves

* **The Feast of Lupercal** The fertility festival of Lupercal was held each year on February 15 in honor of Lupercus. On this day, goats were sacrificed by the priests in charge, who then cut thongs (thin leather strips) from the goatskin. For more information about the festival, see page 30.

Setting the Scene
JULIUS CAESAR
Act I, Scene ii *or* A Dire Warning

Critical Query: What are the complaints against Caesar?

On Location: The Tiber River

The swiftly flowing Tiber is the site of a swimming contest in the next scene. The river winds through Rome and plays a role in the founding of the city. According to legend, a Latin princess gave birth to twins fathered by the god Mars. The princess' father, fearing that the twins, Romulus and Remus, might lay claim to his throne, had the infants put in a basket and set adrift on the Tiber. They were found and nursed by a female wolf, adopted by a shepherd, and eventually built a city (Rome) where they had been abandoned as babies.

Warm-Up Improv

You see two friends talking and you decide to join them. As you approach, they see you and quickly change subjects. You are suspicious and want to know what they were talking about.

Behind the Scene: Epilepsy

Epilepsy is a condition of the nervous system that makes people susceptible to seizures. While often slight, the seizures can also cause brief periods of unconsciousness. It is believed that Caesar suffered from this "falling sickness." Many other famous historical figures are believed to have had this condition, including Alexander the Great, Napoleon, Socrates, Vincent Van Gogh, Leonardo Da Vinci, Michelangelo, Charles Dickens, and Agatha Christie.

Classroom Set Design

The procession of Caesar and his followers should come from the back of the room, down the center aisle to the playing area.

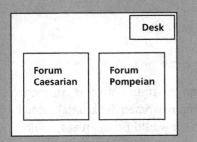

Special Effects

★ Sennet (a trumpet call that indicates an entrance or exit)

★ Flourish (a trumpet fanfare played for emphasis)

Famous Quotes from Scene ii

- Beware the ides of March.
- Men at some time are masters of their fates. The fault, dear Brutus, is not in our stars but in ourselves, that we are underlings.
- Yond Cassius has a lean and hungry look. He thinks too much. Such men are dangerous.
- It was Greek to me.

Caesar enters with his friends, allies, and family. They are enjoying his victory celebrations as well as the traditional Lupercal races. He reminds his wife to stand where the racers can touch her as they pass. It was believed that such a touch could cure infertility. Suddenly a soothsayer (fortune-teller) calls out from the crowd.

Scene ii: Rome. A Public Place

[*Enter* CAESAR, ANTONY (*dressed for the race*), CALPURNIA, PORTIA, DECIUS, CICERO, BRUTUS, CASSIUS, CASCA, A SOOTHSAYER; *after them,* MARULLUS, FLAVIUS, *and* CITIZENS.]

CAESAR. Calpurnia.

CASCA.   Peace, ho! Caesar speaks.

CAESAR.   Calpurnia.

CALPURNIA. Here, my lord.

CAESAR. Stand you directly in Antonius' way
When he doth run his course.—Antonius.

ANTONY. Caesar, my lord.   5

❋ **CAESAR.** Forget not in your speed, Antonius,
To touch Calpurnia, for our elders say
The barren, touchèd in this holy chase,
Shake off their sterile curse.

ANTONY.   I shall remember.
When Caesar says "Do this," it is perform'd.   10

CAESAR. Set on, and leave no ceremony out.

[*Sennet.*]

SOOTHSAYER. Caesar!

CAESAR. Ha! Who calls?

CASCA. Bid every noise be still. Peace yet again!

PERSONA ACTION

Both groups stand in place to watch the procession.

❓ How might Caesar be costumed for his triumphal parade?

PERSONA JOURNAL

How do you celebrate the Lupercal holiday?

8 chase: race

9 sterile curse: curse of infertility

❓ What do lines 9–10 tell you about Antony?

11 Set on: Proceed

Sennet: Trumpet signal

❓ How might Calpurnia react to Caesar's comments about her barrenness? What do these comments tell you about Caesar?

❋ **Race for the Cure** During the feast of Lupercal, young men raced through the streets of Rome, striking spectators with leather straps. Although this might sound rather painful, many women deliberately stood in the racers' paths. According to Roman superstition, being struck by a racer would bring an easy childbirth to pregnant women and help infertile women become pregnant.

Louis Calhern as Caesar and John Gielgud as Cassius with the Soothsayer

The soothsayer cautions Caesar about possible danger on March 15. Caesar scoffs at the warning. Everyone moves on except Brutus and Cassius. Cassius asks Brutus if he intends to watch the races. Brutus replies that he is going home and tells Cassius to go on without him.

CAESAR. Who is it in the press that calls on me?   15
    I hear a tongue shriller than all the music
 ✳ Cry "Caesar." Speak. Caesar is turned to hear.

SOOTHSAYER. Beware the ides of March.

CAESAR.   What man is that?

BRUTUS. A soothsayer bids you beware the ides of March.

CAESAR. Set him before me. Let me see his face.   20

CASSIUS. Fellow, come from the throng.

[The SOOTHSAYER *comes forward.]*

                Look upon Caesar.

CAESAR. What say'st thou to me now? Speak once again.

SOOTHSAYER. Beware the ides of March.

CAESAR. He is a dreamer. Let us leave him. Pass.

[Sennet. Exeunt all but BRUTUS *and* CASSIUS.*]*

CASSIUS. Will you go see the order of the course?   25

BRUTUS. Not I.

CASSIUS. I pray you, do.

BRUTUS. I am not gamesome. I do lack some part
    Of that quick spirit that is in Antony.
    Let me not hinder, Cassius, your desires.   30
    I'll leave you.

15 press: crowd

18 ides: the middle day of the month; in this case, March 15.

PERSONA JOURNAL

Caesar dismisses the soothsayer and his warning. Would you do the same, or are you more superstitious?

PERSONA ACTION

All personas are seated.

25 the order of the course: the running of the race

28 not gamesome: not fond of sports

29 quick: lively

✳ **"Caesar is turned to hear,"** says Caesar when the soothsayer calls out to him. In the play, Caesar often refers to himself in the third person—that is, as "he," "him," or "Caesar," rather than as "I" or "me." In fact, he says his own name 19 times. This sounds pretty egotistical of him. But note that other characters talk like this too. Cassius calls himself "Cassius" 14 times, and Brutus calls himself "Brutus" 13 times. Shakespeare's Rome is full of outsized egos.

Cassius asks Brutus if something is wrong, as Brutus has seemed distracted of late. Brutus confesses that he has been troubled and that he has not meant to annoy or concern his friends with his personal problems.

CASSIUS. Brutus, I do observe you now of late.
   I have not from your eyes that gentleness
   And show of love as I was wont to have.
   You bear too stubborn and too strange a hand   35
   Over your friend that loves you.

BRUTUS.   Cassius,
   Be not deceiv'd. If I have veil'd my look,
   I turn the trouble of my countenance
   Merely upon myself. Vexèd I am
   Of late with passions of some difference,   40
   Conceptions only proper to myself,
   Which give some soil, perhaps, to my behaviours.
   But let not therefore my good friends be griev'd
   (Among which number, Cassius, be you one)
   Nor construe any further my neglect   45
   Than that poor Brutus, with himself at war,
   Forgets the shows of love to other men.

CASSIUS. Then, Brutus, I have much mistook your passion,
   By means whereof this breast of mine hath buried
   Thoughts of great value, worthy cogitations.   50
   Tell me, good Brutus, can you see your face?

BRUTUS. No, Cassius, for the eye sees not itself
   But by reflection, by some other things.

---

32 now of late: lately

34 was wont to have: used to have

35–36 You bear … you: You have been too harsh and too unfriendly with your friend who loves you.

37–39 If I … myself: If I have seemed unfriendly, it is because I have been troubled by my own problems.

39 Vexèd: Upset

40 passions of some difference: conflicting emotions

41 Conceptions only proper to myself: Thoughts that I must keep to myself

42 soil: blemish

45 construe: interpret

48 mistook your passion: mistaken your troubles

49 By means … buried: I have therefore kept to myself

50 cogitations: speculations

Cassius offers to be a "mirror" so that Brutus can see his troubles more clearly. Brutus becomes suspicious about the direction of the conversation, but Cassius asks Brutus to hear him out. They are suddenly interrupted by trumpets and shouts coming from Caesar's victory celebrations.

CASSIUS. 'Tis just.
    And it is very much lamented, Brutus, 55
✱ That you have no such mirrors as will turn
    Your hidden worthiness into your eye,
    That you might see your shadow. I have heard
    Where many of the best respect in Rome
    (Except immortal Caesar), speaking of Brutus 60
    And groaning underneath this age's yoke,
    Have wish'd that noble Brutus had his eyes.

BRUTUS. Into what dangers would you lead me, Cassius,
    That you would have me seek into myself
    For that which is not in me? 65

CASSIUS. Therefore, good Brutus, be prepar'd to hear.
    And since you know you cannot see yourself
    So well as by reflection, I, your glass,
    Will modestly discover to yourself
    That of yourself which you yet know not of. 70
    And be not jealous on me, gentle Brutus.
    Were I a common laugher, or did use
    To stale with ordinary oaths my love
    To every new protester; if you know
    That I do fawn on men and hug them hard 75
    And after scandal them; or if you know
    That I profess myself in banqueting
    To all the rout, then hold me dangerous.

[Flourish and shout.]

54 just: true

55–58 And … shadow: It's too bad that you can't see your own value.

59 best respect: most respected people

61 age's yoke: the burden of these times

62 had his eyes: was not blind to the situation

68 glass: mirror

69–70 modestly discover to yourself/That: frankly reveal to you that part

71 jealous on: suspicious of

72–78 Were I … dangerous: If I were an ordinary fool, or were accustomed, with drunkard's tearful vows, to return affection with everyone who professes love for me; if you know that I shamelessly flatter men and pretend to love them, then afterward slander them; or if you know that, while banqueting, I promise friendship to everyone indiscriminately—then consider me dangerous.

? At this point, which character appeals to you most — Brutus or Cassius? Why?

PERSONA ACTION

When Cassius finishes his speech, a trumpet is heard and a group of Caesarians shout in celebration.

✱ **Self-Reflection** The Romans of Caesar's time knew how to make crude mirrors with glass and metal. But mirrors largely disappeared during the Middle Ages (about 500 A.D. to 1500 A.D.). Around Shakespeare's time, they reappeared in a more sophisticated form—flat sheets of glass backed with tin or silver leaf. Mirrors became very popular in everyday life and in literature. For example, an influential work about English history published in 1559 was entitled *The Mirror for Magistrates.*

Cassius and Brutus fear that Caesar might become their king (thus ending the republic). Brutus declares that he would do anything for the good of the republic as long as it is honorable. Cassius replies that he does not want to live under the rule of someone no better than he is. To make his point, Cassius begins a story about a swimming race between him and Caesar.

BRUTUS. What means this shouting? I do fear the people
  Choose Caesar for their king.

CASSIUS.   Ay, do you fear it?   80
  Then must I think you would not have it so.

BRUTUS. I would not, Cassius, yet I love him well.
  But wherefore do you hold me here so long?
  What is it that you would impart to me?
  If it be aught toward the general good,   85
  Set honour in one eye and death i' th' other
  And I will look on both indifferently;
  For let the gods so speed me as I love
  The name of honour more than I fear death.

CASSIUS. I know that virtue to be in you, Brutus,   90
  As well as I do know your outward favour.
  Well, honour is the subject of my story.
  I cannot tell what you and other men
  Think of this life; but, for my single self,
  I had as lief not be as live to be   95
  In awe of such a thing as I myself.
  I was born free as Caesar; so were you;
  We both have fed as well, and we can both
  Endure the winter's cold as well as he.
✱ For once, upon a raw and gusty day,   100
  The troubled Tiber chafing with her shores,
  Caesar said to me, "Dar'st thou, Cassius, now
  Leap in with me into this angry flood
  And swim to yonder point?" Upon the word,
  Accoutred as I was, I plungèd in   105
  And bade him follow; so indeed he did.

84 impart: tell

85 aught toward the general good: anything for the good of the people

87 indifferently: equally

88 so speed me: so favor me

91 favour: appearance

94 single: individual

95–96 I had … myself: I would just as soon not be alive as live to be afraid of another man no better than myself.

101 chafing with: beating against

102 Dar'st thou: Do you dare

105 Accoutred: Dressed

✱ **Time Trials** Cassius here tells a story of Caesar's humiliation in a swimming match. But Shakespeare made this incident up. Historians record that Caesar was actually an excellent swimmer, even while carrying a stack of books. So why does Shakespeare have Cassius say otherwise? Does Shakespeare want to emphasize Caesar's age? Or is Cassius himself lying in order to win Brutus to his cause?

Cassius continues his story, which paints Caesar as weak, cowardly, and unworthy of the crowd's adoration. As Cassius finishes, another wave of shouts and trumpets is heard.

The torrent roar'd, and we did buffet it
With lusty sinews, throwing it aside
And stemming it with hearts of controversy.
But ere we could arrive the point propos'd,   110
Caesar cried "Help me, Cassius, or I sink!"
I, as Aeneas, our great ancestor,
Did from the flames of Troy upon his shoulder
The old Anchises bear, so from the waves of Tiber
Did I the tired Caesar. And this man   115
Is now become a god, and Cassius is
A wretched creature, and must bend his body
If Caesar carelessly but nod on him.
He had a fever when he was in Spain,
And when the fit was on him, I did mark   120
How he did shake. 'Tis true, this god did shake.
His coward lips did from their color fly,
And that same eye whose bend doth awe the world
Did lose his luster. I did hear him groan.
Ay, and that tongue of his that bade the Romans   125
Mark him, and write his speeches in their books,
"Alas!" it cried, "Give me some drink, Titinius,"
As a sick girl. Ye gods, it doth amaze me
A man of such a feeble temper should
So get the start of the majestic world,   130
And bear the palm alone.

[Shout. Flourish.]

BRUTUS. Another general shout!
I do believe that these applauses are
For some new honours that are heaped on Caesar.

107–108 buffet it/With lusty sinews: swim against it with strong muscles

109 hearts of controversy: our competitive spirit

110 ere: before

112–114 Aeneas founded Rome. This reference is to the legend that Aeneas rescued his father Anchises by carrying him away from the burning city of Troy.

❓ How would Cassius animate his speech in telling this story?

117 bend his body: bow

120 the fit was on him: his temperature climbed; **did mark:** saw

122 did from their color fly: turned pale

123 bend: glance

124 his: its

126 Mark: Pay attention to

129 feeble temper: weak character

130 get the start of: surpass the rest

131 bear the palm: carry the victor's trophy

PERSONA ACTION

Caesarians shout again when given the signal.

CASSIUS. Why, man, he doth bestride the narrow world   135
✱ Like a Colossus, and we petty men
   Walk under his huge legs and peep about
   To find ourselves dishonourable graves.
   Men at some time are masters of their fates.
   The fault, dear Brutus, is not in our stars,   140
   But in ourselves, that we are underlings.
   "Brutus" and "Caesar"—what should be in that "Caesar"?
   Why should that name be sounded more than yours?
   Write them together, yours is as fair a name;
   Sound them, it doth become the mouth as well;   145
   Weigh them, it is as heavy. Conjure with 'em:
   "Brutus" will start a spirit as soon as "Caesar."
   Now, in the names of all the gods at once,
   Upon what meat doth this our Caesar feed
   That he is grown so great? Age, thou art sham'd!   150
   Rome, thou hast lost the breed of noble bloods!
   When went there by an age, since the great flood,
   But it was fam'd with more than with one man?
   When could they say, till now, that talk'd of Rome,
   That her wide walks encompass'd but one man?   155
   Now is it Rome indeed, and room enough
   When there is in it but one only man.
   O, you and I have heard our fathers say
   There was a Brutus once that would have brook'd
   Th' eternal devil to keep his state in Rome   160
   As easily as a king.

136 Colossus: a bronze statue of Helios more than 100 feet high, whose legs are said to have spanned the harbor at Rhodes

141–143: It's not fate but our own fault that we are so inferior.

146 Conjure: Do magic with them

147 start a spirit: call up a ghost

150 Age, thou art sham'd: This generation should be ashamed!

152 the great flood: the secular version of Noah's flood

153 fam'd with: famous for

155 walks encompass'd: streets had room for

156 Rome indeed, and room: During Shakespeare's time, Rome and room were pronounced the same.

159 Brutus: Lucius Junis Brutus, the legendary ancestor of Marcus Brutus, who led a rebellion in 509 B.C. that successfully established the Roman republic form of government

159 brook'd: allowed

❓ In your opinion, is Cassius only concerned about the Roman republic or might there be another reason for his intense dislike of Caesar?

✱ **The Colossus of Rhodes** Cassius here refers to the Colossus of Rhodes in Greece. This bronze statue of the sun god Helios was 100 feet tall. It took 12 years to build and was completed around 280 B.C. The Colossus was toppled by an earthquake around 225 B.C., and its bronze was eventually sold for scrap. According to legend, its legs straddled the entrance to the harbor at Rhodes, but in reality, the statue was not nearly that big. Nevertheless, the Colossus was ranked among the Seven Wonders of the Ancient World.

Brutus ends the conversation promising to consider what Cassius has said. When Caesar and his followers approach, they notice that Caesar and those close to him do not look happy.

BRUTUS. That you do love me, I am nothing jealous.
What you would work me to, I have some aim.
How I have thought of this, and of these times,
I shall recount hereafter. For this present,   165
I would not (so with love I might entreat you)
Be any further mov'd. What you have said
I will consider; what you have to say
I will with patience hear, and find a time
Both meet to hear and answer such high things.   170
Till then, my noble friend, chew upon this:
Brutus had rather be a villager
Than to repute himself a son of Rome
Under these hard conditions as this time
Is like to lay upon us.   175

CASSIUS. I am glad that my weak words
Have struck but thus much show of fire from Brutus.

[Enter CAESAR *and his* TRAIN.*]*

BRUTUS. The games are done, and Caesar is returning.

✱ CASSIUS. As they pass by, pluck Casca by the sleeve,
And he will (after his sour fashion) tell you   180
What hath proceeded worthy note today.

BRUTUS. I will do so. But look you, Cassius,
The angry spot doth glow on Caesar's brow,
And all the rest look like a chidden train.
Calpurnia's cheek is pale, and Cicero   185
Looks with such ferret and such fiery eyes
As we have seen him in the Capitol,
Being cross'd in conference by some senators.

162 I am nothing jealous: I have no doubt

163 aim: guess

166 entreat: ask

167 mov'd: urged

170 meet: appropriate

173 repute: call

175 like: likely

PERSONA ACTION

A group of Caesarians enter with Caesar as his followers and attendants.

TRAIN: group of followers

184 chidden: scolded

186 ferret: red

188 cross'd: disagreed with

✱ **Anachronism** Cassius tells Brutus to "pluck Casca by the sleeve." Actually, Roman statesmen of Caesar's time wore togas, which didn't have sleeves. Togas were oval sheets draped carefully over the body. This kind of historical mistake is called an *anachronism*, and Shakespeare's plays contain many of them. The actors in Shakespeare's original production of *Julius Caesar* probably wore an odd mix of Roman and Elizabethan clothing.

As he passes Cassius and Brutus, Caesar tells Antony that he does not trust Cassius.

Act I   Scene ii

CASSIUS. Casca will tell us what the matter is.

CAESAR. Antonius.   190

ANTONY. Caesar.

✳ CAESAR. Let me have men about me that are fat,
        Sleek-headed men, and such as sleep a-nights.
        Yond Cassius has a lean and hungry look.
        He thinks too much. Such men are dangerous.   195

John Gielgud as
Cassius in the 1953
Mankiewicz film

✳ **Looking for a Few Fat Men** Shakespeare based *Julius Caesar* on parts of *Parallel Lives*, a collection of biographies by the Greek historian Plutarch (c.46–120 A.D.). Shakespeare's language often echoes words, phrases, and descriptions from Plutarch. For example, according to Plutarch, Caesar preferred well-fed men like Antony over slender men like Cassius: "'As for those fat men and smooth-combed heads,' quoth he, 'I never reckon of them: but these pale-visaged and carrion lean people, I fear them most.'"

Caesar continues his conversation with Antony, saying that while he fears no man, if he did fear someone, it would be Cassius. Brutus stops Casca and asks him to relate what has taken place at the festivities.

ANTONY. Fear him not, Caesar; he's not dangerous.
　　He is a noble Roman, and well given.

197 well given: friendly

CAESAR. Would he were fatter! But I fear him not.
　　Yet if my name were liable to fear,
　　I do not know the man I should avoid   200
　　So soon as that spare Cassius. He reads much,
　　He is a great observer, and he looks
　　Quite through the deeds of men. He loves no plays,
　　As thou dost, Antony; he hears no music;
　　Seldom he smiles, and smiles in such a sort   205
　　As if he mock'd himself and scorned his spirit
　　That could be mov'd to smile at anything.
　　Such men as he be never at heart's ease
　　Whiles they behold a greater than themselves,
　　And therefore are they very dangerous.   210
　　I rather tell thee what is to be fear'd
　　Than what I fear; for always I am Caesar.
　　Come on my right hand, for this ear is deaf,
　　And tell me truly what thou think'st of him.

199 Yet if ... fear: Yet, if I were to fear any man

202–203 looks/Quite through: is a sharp observer of

205 sort: way

209 a greater: someone greater

213 on my right hand: move to my right side

[*Sennet. Exeunt* CASCA *and his* TRAIN, *but* CASCA *remains.*]

CASCA. You pull'd me by the cloak. Would you speak with me?   215

BRUTUS. Ay, Casca. Tell us what hath chanc'd today
　　That Caesar looks so sad.

CASCA. Why, you were with him, were you not?

BRUTUS. I should not then ask Casca what had chanc'd.

❓ Why might Caesar fear Cassius?

PERSONA ACTION

Caesar's followers and attendants leave. Be sure to stay in character.

216 chanc'd: happened

217 sad: troubled

Casca says that Caesar was offered a crown three times and each time he rejected it although, in Casca's opinion, he secretly wanted it. Then, continues Casca, Caesar suddenly fainted.

CASCA. Why, there was a crown offered him; and, being   220
offer'd him, he put it by with the back of his hand, thus,
and then the people fell a-shouting.

BRUTUS. What was the second noise for?

CASCA. Why, for that too.

CASSIUS. They shouted thrice. What was the last cry for?   225

CASCA. Why, for that too.

BRUTUS. Was the crown offered him thrice?

CASCA. Ay, marry, was't, and he put it by thrice, every time
gentler than other; and at every putting-by mine honest
neighbors shouted.   230

CASSIUS. Who offered him the crown?

CASCA. Why, Antony.

BRUTUS. Tell us the manner of it, gentle Casca.

CASCA. I can as well be hanged as tell the manner of it. It was
mere foolery; I did not mark it. I saw Mark Antony offer   235
him a crown (yet 'twas not a crown neither; 'twas one of
these coronets) and, as I told you, he put it by once; but
for all that, to my thinking, he would fain have had it.
Then he offered it to him again; then he put it by again;
but to my thinking, he was very loath to lay his fingers off   240
it. And then he offered it the third time. He put it the
third time by, and still as he refused it the rabblement
hooted, and clapped their chopt hands and threw up
their sweaty nightcaps and uttered such a deal of stinking
breath because Caesar refused the crown that it had   245
almost choked Caesar, for he swooned and fell down at it.

221 put it by: pushed it away

225 thrice: three times, yet stage directions only call for Brutus and Cassius to hear the crowd shout two times (pages 34 and 36).

❓ If you were to insert another shout into the action of the play, where would you have it take place?

228 marry, was't: indeed it was. Marry was an oath sworn on the name of the Virgin Mary

PERSONA JOURNAL

What do you think about Caesar being offered the crown?

❓ Why do you think Caesar refused the crown?

233 gentle: noble or amiable

235 mark: pay attention to

237 coronets: small crowns or wreaths

238 fain: gladly

❓ How would you say Casca's lines to convey that he enjoys gossiping?

243 chopt: chapped

246 swooned: fainted

Brutus notes that Caesar suffers from epilepsy. Casca goes on to say that before he fainted, Caesar, in dramatic fashion, offered his bare throat to be cut by any person he might have displeased. And, when he came to, he apologized to anyone he might have offended during his fainting spell.

And for mine own part, I durst not laugh for fear of
opening my lips and receiving the bad air.

CASSIUS. But soft, I pray you. What, did Caesar swoon?

CASCA. He fell down in the market place and foamed at the   250
mouth and was speechless.

BRUTUS. 'Tis very like; he hath the falling sickness.

CASSIUS. No, Caesar hath it not; but you and I
✱ And honest Casca, we have the falling sickness.

CASCA. I know not what you mean by that, but I am sure   255
Caesar fell down. If the tag-rag people did not clap him
and hiss him, according as he pleased and displeased
them, as they use to do the players in the theater, I am no
true man.

BRUTUS. What said he when he came unto himself?   260

CASCA. Marry, before he fell down, when he perceived the
common herd was glad he refused the crown, he plucked
me ope his doublet and offered them his throat to cut.
And I had been a man of any occupation, if I would not
have taken him at a word, I would I might go to hell   265
among the rogues. And so he fell. When he came to
himself again, he said, if he had done or said anything
amiss, he desired their worships to think it was his
infirmity. Three or four wenches where I stood cried,
"Alas, good soul!" and forgave him with all their hearts.   270
But there's no heed to be taken of them; if Caesar had
stabbed their mothers, they would have done no less.

247 durst not: didn't dare

PERSONA JOURNAL

You saw Caesar faint. What was your reaction to it? How did those around you react?

249 But soft: But wait a minute

252 Tis' very … sickness: It's very likely. He has epilepsy.

❓ Why does Cassius say that he and Casca have the falling sickness instead of Caesar?

256 tag-rag people: ragged mob

258 use to: usually

262–263 plucked/me ope his doublet: pulled open his jacket

❓ Can you find an anachronism in lines 262–263?

264 And I … occupation: If I had been a more industrious man

268 amiss: wrong; **their worships:** the good people

269 wenches: girls

271 no heed … them: no need to pay any attention to them

❓ How does Casca's character compare to those of Cassius and Brutus?

✱ **The Falling Sickness** Julius Caesar was far from the only famous person of antiquity to suffer from "the falling sickness," or epilepsy. The ancient Greek philosophers Pythagoras (c.580–c.500 B.C.) and Socrates (c.470–399 B.C.) were thought to have suffered from it too. So did the brilliant Macedonian general Alexander the Great (356–323 B.C.), who conquered much of the known world of his time.

Brutus asks why Caesar looked so serious, but Casca can't answer because Caesar, Cicero, and the others began to speak Greek, which Casca does not understand. He does, however, have other news: the tribunes, Flavius and Marullus have been punished for removing decorations from Caesar's statues.

BRUTUS. And after that, he came thus sad away?

CASCA. Ay.

CASSIUS. Did Cicero say anything?   275

CASCA. Ay, he spoke Greek.

CASSIUS. To what effect?

CASCA. Nay, an I tell you that, I'll ne'er look you i' th' face
again. But those that understood him smiled at one
another and shook their heads. But for mine own part, it   280
★ was Greek to me. I could tell you more news too: Marullus
and Flavius, for pulling scarves off Caesar's images, are put
to silence. Fare you well. There was more foolery yet, if I
could remember it.

CASSIUS. Will you sup with me tonight, Casca?   285

CASCA. No, I am promised forth.

CASSIUS. Will you dine with me tomorrow?

CASCA. Ay, if I be alive, and your mind hold, and your dinner
worth the eating.

CASSIUS. Good. I will expect you.   290

CASCA. Do so. Farewell both.

[Exit.]

BRUTUS. What a blunt fellow is this grown to be!
He was quick mettle when he went to school.

278 an: if

282–283 put/to silence: forced to keep quiet, or possibly, executed

285 sup: dine

288 your mind hold: you don't change your mind

293 quick mettle: sharp

★ **Proverbial Shakespeare** Shakespeare's plays are full of phrases and expressions that are still in common use today. For example, when people hear something they don't understand, they often say, like Casca, "It was Greek to me." Unlike many of Shakespeare's quotable lines, this expression may have been popular even before he wrote *Julius Caesar*.

43

**Brutus and Cassius feel confident that Casca is on their side.
They make plans to meet at a later time and depart.**

CASSIUS. So is he now in execution
    Of any bold or noble enterprise,   295
    However he puts on this tardy form.
    This rudeness is a sauce to his good wit,
    Which gives men stomach to digest his words
    With better appetite.

BRUTUS. And so it is. For this time I will leave you.   300
    Tomorrow, if you please to speak with me,
    I will come home to you; or, if you will,
    Come home to me, and I will wait for you.

CASSIUS. I will do so. Till then, think of the world.

[Exit BRUTUS.*]*

296 puts on this tardy form: pretends to be slow and stupid

304 of the world: about the political situation in Rome

? What do you think Cassius is planning?

Julian Glover as Cassius and John Nettles as Brutus.
Barbican Theatre (London), 1996.

Alone, Cassius wonders how easy it will be to turn the "honorable" Brutus against Caesar. He decides to forge some letters to help convince Brutus to act.

✱ Well, Brutus, thou art noble. Yet I see   305
   Thy honourable mettle may be wrought
   From that it is dispos'd. Therefore 'tis meet
   That noble minds keep ever with their likes;
   For who so firm that cannot be seduc'd?
   Caesar doth bear me hard, but he loves Brutus.   310
   If I were Brutus now, and he were Cassius,
   He should not humour me. I will this night
   In several hands in at his windows throw,
   As if they came from several citizens,
   Writings, all tending to the great opinion   315
   That Rome holds of his name, wherein obscurely
   Caesar's ambition shall be glancèd at.
   And after this, let Caesar seat him sure,
   For we shall shake him, or worse days endure.

   [Exit.]

306 mettle may be wrought: nature can be altered

307 meet: proper

310 doth bear me hard: is against me

312 He should not humour me: He would not be able to persuade me.

313 In several ... throw: forge some letters using different handwritings and throw them in Brutus' window

315 great opinion: great respect

316 obscurely: secretly

317 glancèd: hinted

318 seat him sure: make sure of his position

❓ How does Cassius plan to convince Brutus to join his plot?

❓ What might Cassius write in these anonymous letters to Brutus?

✱ **Monologues and soliloquies** are both long speeches delivered by a single actor. So what's the difference between them? A monologue can be delivered to other characters. A soliloquy expresses a character's private thoughts. Cassius' speech that closes this scene is a soliloquy, in which he describes his plans to manipulate Brutus. Although Shakespeare didn't invent the soliloquy, he used it more brilliantly than any other writer before or since to reveal the innermost thoughts of his characters.

Setting the Scene

JULIUS CAESAR

Act I, Scene iii *or* The Plot Thickens

Critical Query: What actions are being planned?

Warm-Up Improv

You are a car salesperson and your dealership is having a contest. There's a terrific prize waiting for the person who sells the most automobiles. You are pushing an unsure customer using flattery, facts—anything to close the deal. In the background you hear cheers from others as they make sales. You become nervous and worried that they are getting ahead of you.

On Location: Pompey's Porch

In 55 B.C. Pompey built a theatre complex in Rome that seated thousands of spectators. The porch of the building, where people could seek shelter, was said to have one hundred columns.

Time Capsule: The Praetor's Chair

A *praetor* was a consul or judge in ancient Rome. Shortly before the action of this play, Brutus was named a praetor by Caesar. Praetors sat in special chairs as they judged disputes.

Special ffects

- Thunder (intermittently throughout the scene)
- Lightning (can be achieved by flicking classroom lights on and off)

From the Prop Box

- Dagger for Cassius
- Letters

Classroom Set Design

This is the standard setup with two forums and a playing area at the front of the classroom.

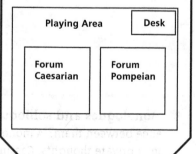

Playing Area	Desk
Forum Caesarian	Forum Pompeian

Who's Who? Cicero

Marcus Tullius Cicero (106–43 B.C.) was a philosopher and senator especially known for his powerful speeches. For the most part he admired Caesar. Though not one of the conspirators, he was nevertheless considered an enemy by the triumvirate that ruled after Caesar's death. He was murdered in 43 B.C.

Casca and Cicero greet each other on the street during a violent thunderstorm. Casca is fearful of the unnatural events that have been occurring.

Scene iij: Rome, A Street

✱ *[Thunder and lightning. Enter* CASCA *and* CICERO *at different doors.]*

CICERO. Good even, Casca, Brought you Caesar home?
　　Why are you breathless, and why stare you so?

CASCA. Are not you mov'd, when all the sway of earth
　　Shakes like a thing unfirm? O Cicero,
　　I have seen tempests when the scolding winds　　　　5
　　Have riv'd the knotty oaks, and I have seen
　　Th' ambitious ocean swell and rage and foam
　　To be exalted with the threat'ning clouds;
　　But never till tonight, never till now,
　　Did I go through a tempest
　　dropping fire.　　　　　　　　　　　　　　　　10
　　Either there is a civil
　　strife in heaven,
　　Or else the world,
　　too saucy with the gods,
　　Incenses them to
　　send destruction.

Engraving of Casca and Cicero.
Kenny Meadows, 1846.

❓ Describe the lighting and sound effects you might plan for this scene.

PERSONA ACTION

As the scene opens, various personas stand in place reacting to the severe weather and strange sights in Rome. As Cicero and Casca begin to speak, the persona voices should fade into pantomime. Personas then sit quietly as the scene continues.

1 even: evening; **Brought you:** Did you escort

3 all the sway: the entire

5 tempests: storms; **scolding:** raging

6 riv'd: split

8 exalted with: raised up to

12 saucy: insolent

✱ **Special Effects** To create flashes of lightning, Shakespeare's stagehands ignited black powder, a chemical used in early firearms. To produce thunder-like noises, they shook huge metal sheets and possibly rolled cannon balls down a chute. A similar technique for thunder was used during the 19th century with the cannon balls being piled into a wheelbarrow and rolled over an uneven surface. One over-zealous stagehand managed to tip over the barrow, sending cannonballs careening onto the stage.

Casca describes strange sights. Cicero acknowledges that such things have been happening, but points out that these omens could have many meanings. Casca tells Cicero that Caesar will be at the Capitol the next day.

CICERO. Why, saw you anything more <u>wonderful</u>?

CASCA. A common slave—you know him well by sight—   15
   Held up his left hand, which did flame and burn
   Like twenty torches join'd; and yet his hand,
   <u>Not sensible of fire</u>, remain'd unscorch'd.
   Besides—I ha' not since put up my sword—
   Against the Capitol I met a lion,   20
   Who glaz'd upon me, and went surly by
   Without annoying me. And there were drawn
   Upon a heap a hundred ghastly women,
   Transformèd with their fear, who swore they saw
   Men all in fire walk up and down the streets.   25
   And yesterday the bird of night did sit
   Even at noonday upon the market place,
   Hooting and shrieking. When these prodigies
   Do so conjointly meet, let not men say
   "These are their reasons, they are natural,"   30
   For I believe they are portentous things
   Unto the climate that they point upon.

CICERO. Indeed, it is a strange-disposèd time.
   But men may construe things after their fashion,
   Clean from the purpose of the things themselves.   35
   Comes Caesar to the Capitol tomorrow?

CASCA. He doth, for he did bid Antonius
   Send word to you he would be there tomorrow.

---

14 wonderful: amazing

18 Not sensible of fire: Not feeling the fire

19 ha': have

20 Against: Opposite

21 glaz'd upon: stared at

22 annoying: harming

22–23 drawn/Upon a heap: huddled together

26 bird of night: owl

28 prodigies: incredible events

29 so conjointly meet: all occur together

31 portentous: threatening

32 climate: region

33 a strange-disposèd: an abnormal

34–35 construe things ... themselves: interpret things as they please, which may be the opposite of their actual meanings.

Foreshadowing in literature refers to hints about what will occur later in the plot. The wild weather and unnatural events described by Cicero, Casca, and Cassius seem to portend future disruption and chaos. As you read, be on the lookout for other clues that might foretell the future.

Cassius and Casca also speak about the storm. Casca continues to be fearful.

CICERO. Good night then, Casca. This disturbèd sky
    Is not to walk in.

CASCA.   Farewell, Cicero.   40

[Exit CICERO.]

[Enter CASSIUS.]

CASSIUS. Who's there?

CASCA.   A Roman.

✴ CASSIUS.   Casca, by your voice.

CASCA. Your ear is good. Cassius, what night is this!

CASSIUS. A very pleasing night to honest men.

CASCA. Who ever knew the heavens menace so?

CASSIUS. Those that have known the earth so full of faults.   45
    For my part, I have walk'd about the streets,
    Submitting me unto the perilous night,
    And thus unbracèd, Casca, as you see,
    Have bar'd my bosom to the thunder-stone;
    And when the cross blue lightning seem'd to open   50
    The breast of heaven, I did present myself
    Even in the aim and very flash of it.

CASCA. But wherefore did you so much tempt the heavens?
    It is the part of men to fear and tremble
    When the most mighty gods by tokens send   55
    Such dreadful heralds to astonish us.

CASSIUS. You are dull, Casca, and those sparks of life
    That should be in a Roman you do want,
    Or else you use not. You look pale, and gaze,

PERSONA JOURNAL

What have you seen and heard during this strange, stormy night?

48 unbracèd: with unbuttoned jacket

49 thunder-stone: thunderbolt

50 cross: forked

54 part: nature

✴ **"Casca, by your voice."** Remember that *Julius Caesar* was originally performed in the open air in afternoon daylight. This made night scenes a challenge to the audience's imagination. Actors sometimes carried torches to suggest darkness. And lines of dialogue often suggested the difficulty of seeing in the dark—as when Cassius claims to be able to identify Casca only by his voice.

Cassius refuses to be frightened and claims that nature's violence is sending a warning about Caesar and his ambitions. Casca then tells Cassius that the Senate intends to make Caesar king the next day.

And put on fear, And cast yourself in wonder,   60
To see the strange impatience of the heavens.
But if you would consider the true cause
Why all these fires, why all these gliding ghosts,
Why birds and beasts from quality and kind,
Why old men, fools, and children calculate,   65
Why all these things change from their ordinance,
Their natures, and preformèd faculties,
To monstrous quality—why, you shall find
That heaven hath infus'd them with these spirits
To make them instruments of fear and warning   70
Unto some monstrous state.
Now could I, Casca, name to thee a man
Most like this dreadful night,
That thunders, lightens, opens graves, and roars
✱ As doth the lion in the Capitol;   75
A man no mightier than thyself or me
In personal action, yet prodigious grown,
And fearful, as these strange eruptions are.

CASCA. 'Tis Caesar that you mean, is it not, Cassius?

CASSIUS. Let it be who it is. For Romans now   80
Have thews and limbs like to their ancestors.
But, woe the while, our fathers' minds are dead,
And we are govern'd with our mothers' spirits.
Our yoke and sufferance show us womanish.

CASCA. Indeed, they say the Senators tomorrow   85
Mean to establish Caesar as a king,
And he shall wear his crown by sea and land
In every place save here in Italy.

60 cast yourself in wonder: throw yourself into a state of amazement

64 from quality and kind: are behaving so differently from their nature

65 calculate: prophesize

66–68 change from ... quality: turn away from their established order, their natures, and inherent qualities and are transformed into something monstrous

78 fearful: frightful

81 Have thews and limbs like: Are still strong like

82 woe the while: alas for this generation; **fathers' minds are:** ancestors' strong manly spirit is

84 yoke and sufferance: meek acceptance of tyranny

✱ **Lions in London** In 1599, when *Julius Caesar* was first presented, lions were being kept in the Tower of London, an ancient fortress across the Thames from the Globe Theatre. Shakespeare may have had these lions in mind when he had Cassius refer to a "lion in the Capitol."

The idea of Caesar as king infuriates Cassius; he declares he would rather kill himself than live under the rule of such a person.

CASSIUS. I know where I will wear this dagger then;
   Cassius from bondage will deliver Cassius.   90
   Therein, ye gods, you make the weak most strong;
   Therein, ye gods, you tyrants do defeat.
   Nor stony tower, nor walls of beaten brass,
   Nor airless dungeon, nor strong links of iron,
   Can be retentive to the strength of spirit;   95
   But life, being weary of these worldly bars,
   Never lacks power to dismiss itself.
   If I know this, know all the world besides,
   That part of tyranny that I do bear
   I can shake off at pleasure.

    [Thunder still.]

89–90 Suicide is implied here.

91 Therein: In suicide

95 Can be retentive: Are powerful enough against

97 dismiss: free

❓ Do you think Cassius would actually commit suicide? Why or why not?

Alex Webb (left) as Casca and Louis Butelli as Cassius. Aquila Theatre Company, 2000.

Casca says that he also has the strength to kill himself, but instead of suicide, Cassius suggests that Casca join him in a plot against Caesar. He also implies that there are other prominent Romans ready to help.

CASCA.   So can I.
So every bondman in his own hand bears   100
The power to cancel his captivity.

CASSIUS. And why should Caesar be a tyrant, then?
✳ Poor man, I know he would not be a wolf
But that he sees the Romans are but sheep;
He were no lion, were not Romans hinds.   105
Those that with haste will make a mighty fire
Begin it with weak straws. What trash is Rome,
What rubbish and what offal, when it serves
For the base matter to illuminate   110
So vile a thing as Caesar! But, O grief,
Where hast thou led me? I perhaps speak this
Before a willing bondman; then, I know
My answer must be made. But I am arm'd,
And dangers are to me indifferent.   115

CASCA. You speak to Casca, and to such a man
That is no fleering telltale. Hold. My hand.

[They shake hands.]

Be factious for redress of all these griefs,
And I will set this foot of mine as far
As who goes farthest.

CASSIUS.   There's a bargain made.   120
Now know you, Casca, I have mov'd already
Some certain of the noblest-minded Romans
To undergo with me an enterprise
Of honourable-dangerous consequence.

101 bondman: slave

106 hinds: deer

109 offal: waste or garbage

110 base matter to illuminate: fuel to make famous

❓ Explain the fire metaphor used by Cassius in lines 107–111.

114 My answer must be made: My words shall need to be defended.

117 fleering: sneering; **Hold:** Wait

118 Be factious ... griefs: Let's join together to set right all of our grievances.

121 mov'd: persuaded

✳ **Similes and metaphors** are figures of speech. Similes are comparisons between two unlike things that use the words *like* or *as*; metaphors are also comparisons, but they leave out the words *like* or *as*. Cassius is speaking metaphorically when he says that Caesar "would not be a wolf/But that he sees the Romans are but sheep ..." Cassius would have used similes if he had said, instead, "I know he would not be *like* a wolf/But that he sees the Romans are *like* sheep."

Cinna arrives to tell Casca and Cassius that others are waiting for them. He asks Cassius to convince Brutus to become part of the growing conspiracy against Caesar, and Cassius responds that such plans are already in motion. He enlists Cinna's help in delivering the forged letters to Brutus.

And I do know, by this they stay for me   125
In Pompey's Porch. For now, this fearful night,
There is no stir or walking in the streets;
And the complexion of the element
Is favour'd like the work we have in hand,
Most bloody, fiery, and most terrible.   130

[Enter CINNA.]

CASCA. Stand close awhile, for here comes one in haste.

CASSIUS. 'Tis Cinna; I do know him by his gait.
✷ He is a friend—Cinna, where haste you so?

CINNA. To find out you. Who's that, Metellus Cimber?

CASSIUS. No, it is Casca, one incorporate   135
To our attempts. Am I not stay'd for, Cinna?

CINNA. I am glad on't. What a fearful night is this!
There's two or three of us have seen strange sights.

CASSIUS. Am I not stay'd for? Tell me.

CINNA.   Yes, you are.
O Cassius, if you could   140
but win the noble Brutus to our party—

CASSIUS. Be you content. Good Cinna, take this paper,
And look you lay it in the Praetor's chair,
Where Brutus may but find it; and throw this
In at his window; set this up with wax   145
Upon old Brutus' statue. All this done,
Repair to Pompey's Porch, where you shall find us.
Is Decius Brutus and Trebonius there?

---

125 by this they stay for me: by this time they are waiting for me

126 Pompey's Porch: the colonnade of the theatre built by Pompey

128 complexion of the element: appearance of the sky

131 close: hidden

135–136 one incorporate/To our attempts: someone who is part of the plot

136 Am I not stay'd for: Are they waiting for me?

137 on't: of it

❓ Why does Cinna want Brutus involved with their plot?

143 Praetor's chair: the chair of the chief magistrate

145 set this up with wax: attach this one with wax

146 old Brutus': Brutus' famous ancestor

147 Repair: Come

✷ **What's in a Name?** Note that one of the conspirators is named Cinna, perhaps a common Roman name at the time of the play. This name and a case of mistaken identity will lead to a horrific event later in the play.

Casca, Cinna, and Cassius make plans to join the others who conspire against Caesar and to convince Brutus to unite with them as well.

CINNA. All but Metellus Cimber, and he's gone
    To see you at your house. Well, I will hie   150
    And so bestow these papers as you bade me.

CASSIUS. That done, repair to Pompey's Theater.

[Exit CINNA.]

    Come, Casca, you and I will yet ere day
    See Brutus at his house. Three parts of him
    Is ours already, and the man entire   155
    Upon the next encounter yields him ours.

CASCA. O, he sits high in all the people's hearts,
    And that which would appear offense in us,
✱ His countenance, like richest alchemy,
    Will change to virtue and to worthiness.   160

CASSIUS. Him and his worth and our great need of him
    You have right well conceited. Let us go,
    For it is after midnight, and ere day
    We will awake him and be sure of him.

[Exeunt.]

150 hie: run along

153 ere day: before dawn
154 Three parts: Three-quarters

156 yields him ours: will deliver him to us

159 countenance: approval; **alchemy:** turning base metal into gold

162 right well conceited: judged correctly

PERSONA JOURNAL

Do you hold Brutus in high esteem? Why or why not?

✱ **"His countenance, like richest alchemy ..."** Alchemy was the ancient art of trying to turn metals like tin and lead into gold. Although now regarded as pure pseudoscience, alchemy was still taken seriously in Shakespeare's time. And although alchemists never succeeded in making gold, they achieved useful discoveries that contributed to today's science of chemistry.

Edward Herrmann as Cassius. New York Shakespeare Festival, 1988.

Reacting to Act I

Analysis

1. What do you think is the purpose of the quarrel between the tribunes and the commoners at the beginning of the play?

2. Caesar is suspicious of Cassius. Identify four qualities in Cassius that Caesar does not like.

3. How do we learn what kind of relationship Caesar and Brutus have had?

4. Read Cassius' description of Caesar in Scene ii. What does it tell you about his character as well as Caesar's character?

5. In Scene ii, Casca says that after being offered the crown, Caesar "swooned and fell down." Do you think that Caesar really fainted? Explain why or why not.

6. What is revealed in Cassius' rebuke to Casca during the storm?

7. Why do you think Shakespeare gives Caesar so few lines and so little stage time, even during the scenes in which he appears?

Literary Elements

1. A **pun** is a play on a word that has one sound but more than one possible spelling or meaning. Find a pun in Act I and explain its different meanings. Why do you think Shakespeare used the pun here?

2. **Foreshadowing** refers to hints in the text about what might happen later. What examples of foreshadowing do you find in Act I?

3. A **simile** is a comparison of two unlike things using *like* or *as*. Find a simile in this act. How does it strengthen the description of the person, place, or thing being compared?

4. **Conflict** is the struggle between opposing forces. In this act, identify the different opinions that people—Brutus, Cassius, Casca, and the commoners—have about Caesar's character and role as a Roman ruler. Because of these differences, what conflicts are brewing?

Writing

1. Write a newspaper account of Caesar's refusal of the crown of Rome on the day of the Lupercal festivities. Make sure to interview at least three or four bystanders. Remember: newsreaders expect answers to the questions *Who, What, Where, When,* and, if possible, *Why* or *How.*

2. Look up the word *conspiracy* in the dictionary. Are there ever any good reasons for conspiring to overthrow a ruler or government? Now decide if there are any good reasons for the conspiracy against Caesar. Back up your opinions with examples.

3. Even today, some people believe in superstitions about the weather or animals. For example, you may have heard the saying, "Red sky at morning, sailors take warning." Or, you may know the belief that if a groundhog sees its shadow on February 2, there will be six more weeks of winter. List five or six of these superstitions and then make up one of your own.

Julius Caesar ACT II

Brutus and Portia. Ercole de' Roberti, 1490.

"Dear my lord, make me acquainted with your cause of grief."

Setting the Scene
JULIUS CAESAR

Act II, Scene i *or* Decisions, Decisions

Critical Query: What is Brutus' position regarding Caesar
at the beginning of this scene? At the end?

Who's Who? Brutus

In today's English, the word *brute* has come to refer to a cruel and loutish person. Did this meaning come about because of Brutus' savage killing of Julius Caesar? Not at all. The Latin word *brutus* originally meant "dull" or "stupid." It had this meaning long before the time of Julius Caesar. One of Brutus' ancestors, Lucius Junius Brutus, got his name by pretending to be an idiot in order to save his own life. But this same Brutus redeemed the family name by ridding Rome of its last king, Lucius Tarquinius Superbus, in 509 B.C. Lucius Junius Brutus was also said to have founded the Roman republic, which the Brutus of Shakespeare's play is so determined to preserve against Caesar's tyranny.

Special Effects
- Striking clock
- Thunder

From the Prop Box
- Letter
- Kerchief for Ligarius
- Sword for Casca

Time Capsule: The Julian Calendar

Before 45 B.C. the Roman calendar was so complicated that special officials were needed to keep track of it. These timekeepers decided when to add or subtract days and even months to keep holidays falling in their correct seasons. This arbitrary system was modified by Caesar to reflect a solar year of 365 days with an additional day added every four years—similar to the system we use today. In his honor, the month of Quintilis was renamed Julius (July).

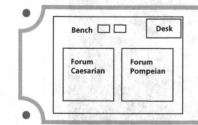

Classroom Set Design

The standard two-forum design with two chairs serving as a bench

Warm-Up Improv 1	Warm-Up Improv 2
You are the top executive of a company that has a position open. A close friend wants the job, but you are concerned that he/she is not quite suitable. To help you decide, you are discussing the situation with the company's personnel director.	Your school football team will play in the state championship game. The team's leading scorer has broken a school rule. The usual punishment requires suspension from athletics. Six of you on the student council are deciding what will happen.

Unable to sleep, Brutus calls for his servant, Lucius, to light a candle in his study. Alone in the garden, he wrestles with his thoughts about Caesar.

ACT II

Scene i. Rome

[Enter BRUTUS *in his orchard.]*

BRUTUS. What, Lucius, ho!—
    I cannot by the progress of the stars
    Give guess how near to day.—Lucius, I say!—
    I would it were my fault to sleep so soundly.—
    When, Lucius, when? Awake, I say! What, Lucius!   5

[Enter LUCIUS.*]*

LUCIUS. Call'd you, my lord?

BRUTUS. Get me a taper in my study, Lucius.
    When it is lighted, come and call me here.

LUCIUS. I will, my lord.

[Exit LUCIUS.*]*

✴ **BRUTUS.** It must be by his death. And for my part   10
    I know no personal cause to spurn at him,
    But for the general. He would be crown'd.
    How that might change his nature, there's the question.
    It is the bright day that brings forth the adder,
    And that craves wary walking. Crown him that,   15
    And then I grant we put a sting in him
    That at his will he may do danger with.
    Th' abuse of greatness is when it disjoins
    Remorse from power. And, to speak truth of Caesar,
    I have not known when his affections sway'd   20

❓ How would you speak the part of Lucius to convey that he was just awakened from a deep sleep?

7 taper: candle

10 his: Caesar's

11 spurn at: oppose

12 But for the general: Except that it would be in the best interests of the public; **would be:** wishes to be

14–17 It is ... with: A sunny day encourages snakes to come out into the open, and forces us to walk very carefully. If we make him king, we give him the kind of power that could be dangerous to us.

18–19 disjoins/Remorse: takes away compassion

20 affections sway'd: emotions ruled

PERSONA JOURNAL

What difference would it make to you if Caesar were crowned king?

✴ **Too Close for Comfort?** Although set in ancient Rome, Shakespeare's *Julius Caesar* may have seemed a bit too real when it was first produced in 1599. England's Queen Elizabeth was, like Shakespeare's Caesar, proud, dictatorial, and aging. And many doubted that there could be a peaceful transfer of royal power after her death. Shakespeare may have modeled the character of Brutus on the rebellious Earl of Essex, who unsuccessfully tried to overthrow the queen a couple of years after *Julius Caesar* was first performed.

Len Cariou as Brutus. Stratford Festival, 1982.

Brutus decides that Caesar's death is necessary. The danger that he would abuse his power if he became king is too great. Lucius returns with a letter he has found in the study.

More than his reason. But 'tis a common proof
That lowliness is young ambition's ladder,
Whereto the climber upward turns his face;
But, when he once attains the upmost round,   25
He then unto the ladder turns his back,
Looks in the clouds, scorning the base degrees
By which he did ascend. So Caesar may.
Then, lest he may, prevent. And since the quarrel
Will bear no colour for the thing he is,
Fashion it thus: that what he is, augmented,   30
Would run to these and these extremities.
And therefore think him as a serpent's egg,
Which, hatch'd, would, as his kind, grow mischievous,
And kill him in the shell.

[Enter LUCIUS.]

LUCIUS. The taper burneth in your closet, sir.   35
Searching the window for a flint, I found
This paper, thus seal'd up, and I am sure
It did not lie there when I went to bed.

[LUCIUS gives him the letter.]

BRUTUS. Get you to bed again. It is not day.
Is not tomorrow, boy, the ides of March?   40

LUCIUS. I know not, sir.

✱ BRUTUS. Look in the calendar and bring me word.

LUCIUS. I will, sir.

[Exit LUCIUS.]

21 **common proof:** often happens

22 **lowliness:** humility

❓ Do you believe that power corrupts?

24 **upmost round:** top rung

26 **base degrees:** lower rungs

❓ Explain the ladder metaphor in lines 21–28.

28–30 **the quarrel … thus:** my quarrel with Caesar cannot be based on what he is now. I must justify it in this way.

31 **run to these and these extremities:** reach many of these extremes

33 **as his kind:** naturally; **mischievous:** malicious

❓ How does Brutus justify killing Caesar? Do you agree with his reasoning?

35 **closet:** study

PERSONA JOURNAL

Have you ever witnessed anything in Caesar's past behavior that would lead you to believe that he would abuse his power? Explain, using examples to support a yes or no answer.

✱ **"Look in the calendar and bring me word,"** Brutus asks Lucius, uncertain of the date. Brutus had reason to be confused. In 46 B.C., two years before his death, Julius Caesar revised the old Roman calendar, which had become very unreliable over the centuries. Maybe Brutus hadn't quite gotten the hang of Caesar's fancy new calendar. Caesar's calendar—called the "Julian Calendar"—remained standard until Shakespeare's time. Then it slowly began to be replaced by the Gregorian calendar, the one we use today.

Brutus reads the letter, which urges him to help protect the republic of Rome. He is reminded of his ancestors who, many years earlier, saved Rome by wresting power from a tyrant king. Brutus believes it is his destiny to do so once again.

BRUTUS. The exhalations, whizzing in the air,
　　Give so much light that I may read by them.　　　45

[Opens the letter and reads.]

　　"Brutus, thou sleep'st. Awake, and see thyself!
　　Shall Rome, etc. Speak, strike, redress!"
　　"Brutus, thou sleep'st. Awake!"
　　Such instigations have been often dropp'd
　　Where I have took them up.　　　　　　　　　50
　　"Shall Rome, etc." Thus must I piece it out:
　　Shall Rome stand under one man's awe? What, Rome?
✱　My ancestors did from the streets of Rome
　　The Tarquin drive when he was call'd a king.
　　"Speak, strike, redress!" Am I entreated　　　55
　　To speak and strike? O Rome, I make thee promise,
　　If the redress will follow, thou receivest
　　Thy full petition at the hand of Brutus.

[Enter LUCIUS.]

LUCIUS. Sir, March is wasted fifteen days.

[Knock within.]

BRUTUS. 'Tis good. Go to the gate; somebody knocks.　60

[Exit LUCIUS.]

　　Since Cassius first did whet me against Caesar,
　　I have not slept.
　　Between the acting of a dreadful thing
　　And the first motion, all the interim is
　　Like a phantasma or a hideous dream.　　　　　65

44 exhalations: meteors

47 redress: make things right

51 piece it out: fill in the blanks

52 under one man's awe: in fear of one man

55 entreated: begged

57–58 If the redress ... Brutus: If good will come from my action, Rome will receive everything that she asks for from the hands of Brutus.

❓ Why do you think Brutus is so concerned with the time and date?

61 whet me: stir me up

❓ Have you ever lost sleep worrying over a decision you needed to make?

64 motion: impulse to do it

65 phantasma: hallucination

✱ **All in the Family** Brutus refers to his famous relative, Junius Brutus. Junius, it is said, overthrew the tyrannical King Tarquin in 509 B.C. and helped to establish the Roman republic. Brutus wonders if he is being called upon to protect the republic founded by his ancestor.

The genius and the mortal instruments
Are then in council, and the state of a man,
Like to a little kingdom, suffers then
The nature of an insurrection.

66–67 The genius ... council: A man's guardian spirit and his physical abilities consult with each other.

[Enter LUCIUS.]

LUCIUS.   Sir, 'tis your brother Cassius at the door, 70
Who doth desire to see you.

70 brother: brother-in-law (Cassius is married to Brutus' sister.)

BRUTUS.   Is he alone?

LUCIUS.   No, sir. There are more with him.

❓ Do you think Brutus is concerned about the identities of these men? Why or why not?

✱ BRUTUS.   Do you know them?

LUCIUS.   No, sir. Their hats are pluck'd about their ears,
And half their faces buried in their cloaks,
That by no means I may discover them 75
By any mark of favour.

75 discover: recognize

76 any mark of favour: their unique features

Brutus with the Conspirators.
Kenny Meadows, 1846.

✱ **Editor's Error** During the 18th century, critics considered Shakespeare an untutored genius whose writings badly needed correction. For example, when the poet Samuel Pope was editing a new collection of Shakespeare's works, he was shocked to find what seemed like an anachronism in Lucius' remark, "their hats are plucked about their ears ..." Pope was just *sure* that Romans never wore hats! So he removed the word "hats" from Lucius' line. But Shakespeare was right—residents of ancient Rome sometimes really did wear hats.

As he waits for his visitors, Brutus reflects on the dark nature of conspiracy. Cassius greets Brutus and introduces the others who have arrived with him. Cassius flatters Brutus and apologizes for having interrupted his sleep.

✳ **BRUTUS.**   Let 'em enter.

[Exit LUCIUS.*]*

> They are the faction. O Conspiracy,
> Sham'st thou to show thy dang'rous brow by night,
> When evils are most free? O, then, by day
> Where wilt thou find a cavern dark enough   80
> To mask thy monstrous visage? Seek none, conspiracy.
> Hide it in smiles and affability;
> For if thou path, thy native semblance on,
> Not Erebus itself were dim enough
> To hide thee from prevention.   85

[Enter the conspirators, CASSIUS, CASCA, DECIUS, CINNA, METELLUS, *and* TREBONIUS.*]*

CASSIUS. I think we are too bold upon your rest.
> Good morrow, Brutus. Do we trouble you?

BRUTUS. I have been up this hour, awake all night.
> Know I these men that come along with you?

CASSIUS. Yes, every man of them; and no man here   90
> But honours you, and every one doth wish
> You had but that opinion of yourself
> Which every noble Roman bears of you.
> This is Trebonius.

BRUTUS.   He is welcome hither.

CASSIUS. This, Decius Brutus.

BRUTUS.   He is welcome too.

---

77 faction: group that opposes Caesar

81 visage: face

82 affability: pleasant manners

83 if thou … on: you revealed yourself as you really are

84 Erebus: in classical mythology, a dark place between Earth and Hades through which the dead pass

85 prevention: being discovered

87 morrow: morning

✳ **Richard Burbage** The role of Brutus was probably originally played by Shakespeare's favorite tragic actor, Richard Burbage. Shakespeare created many of his greatest roles for Burbage. These probably included Richard III, Romeo, Hamlet, Othello, King Lear, and Macbeth. A multitalented man, Burbage was also highly regarded as a portrait painter.

CASSIUS. This, Casca; this, Cinna; and this, Metellus Cimber.

BRUTUS. They are all welcome.
     What watchful cares do interpose themselves
     Betwixt your eyes and night?

CASSIUS. Shall I entreat a word?   100

✱ *[They whisper.]*

DECIUS. Here lies the east; doth not the day break here?

CASCA. No.

CINNA. O pardon, sir, it doth; and yon gray lines
     That fret the clouds are messengers of day.

CASCA. You shall confess that you are both deceiv'd.   105
     Here, as I point my sword, the sun arises,
     Which is a great way growing on the south,
     Weighing the youthful season of the year.
     Some two months hence, up higher toward the north
     He first presents his fire, and the high east   110
     Stands, as the Capitol, directly here.

BRUTUS. *[Coming forward with CASSIUS.]*

     Give me your hands all
     over, one by one.

> 98 **watchful cares:** worries that keep you awake; **interpose:** insert
>
> 99 **Betwixt:** Between
>
> 100 **Shall I entreat a word:** May I have a word with you in private?
>
> ❓ What do you think Cassius and Brutus are saying to each other?
>
> 104 **fret:** intertwine
>
> 107 **growing on:** toward
>
> 108 **Weighing:** Considering
>
> 110 **He:** The sun
>
> 111 **as the Capitol:** as does the Capitol
>
> 112–113 **all over:** everyone

John Wood as Brutus (center) joins hands with the other conspirators in a plot against Caesar. Royal Shakespeare Company, 1972.

✱ **Idle Talk** Here Cassius whispers to Brutus, finally persuading him to take part in the conspiracy. Shakespeare doesn't want us to hear what Cassius and Brutus say, so he "covers" their whispering with insignificant chatter between the other conspirators. Or is this chatter really so insignificant? Notice that Casca points his sword toward the Capitol—where he will be the first of the conspirators to stab Julius Caesar.

Cassius asks the group to swear an oath to seal their pact to assassinate Caesar. Brutus asks that they join hands instead, declaring that their word is enough and an oath is not necessary.

CASSIUS. And let us swear our resolution.

* BRUTUS. No, not an oath. If not the face of men,
The sufferance of our souls, the time's abuse—   115
If these be motives weak, break off betimes,
And every man hence to his idle bed.
So let high-sighted tyranny range on
Till each man drop by lottery. But if these,
(As I am sure they do) bear fire enough   120
To kindle cowards and to steel with valour
The melting spirits of women, then, countrymen,
What need we any spur but our own cause
To prick us to redress? What other bond
Than secret Romans that have spoke the word   125
And will not palter? And what other oath
Than honesty to honesty engag'd
That this shall be or we will fall for it?
Swear priests and cowards and men cautelous,
Old feeble carrions, and such suffering souls   130
That welcome wrongs; unto bad causes swear
Such creatures as men doubt; but do not stain
The even virtue of our enterprise,
Nor th' insuppressive mettle of our spirits,
To think that or our cause or our performance   135
Did need an oath, when every drop of blood
That every Roman bears, and nobly bears,
Is guilty of a several bastardy
If he do break the smallest particle
Of any promise that hath passed from him.   140

114 face of men: troubled looks

115 sufferance: sufferings; **time's abuse:** political abuses of the times

116 betimes: at once

117 hence: go

118 high-sighted: arrogant; **range on:** continue

119 drop by lottery: die by chance; **these:** these motives

124 To pick us to redress: To incite us to correct these conditions

125 secret Romans: Romans able to keep a secret

126 palter: change their minds

127 honesty to honesty engag'd: the personal honor of one man's word to another

128 fall for: die because of

129 men cautelous: crafty men

130 carrions: living carcasses

133 even: pure

134 insuppressive mettle: unbeatable courage

135 or our cause or: either our cause or

138 several bastardy: separate act not of Roman blood

? What reasons does Brutus give for not swearing an oath?

---

* **No Swearing, Please** Shakespeare's historical source, Plutarch's *Lives*, says that the conspirators had never "taken oaths together, nor taken or given any caution or assurance, nor binding themselves one to another by religious oaths ..." Plutarch doesn't say that it was Brutus' idea *not* to take oaths; this is Shakespeare's invention. Note how the playwright uses this small historical detail to emphasize Brutus' idealistic nature.

Cassius, Casca, Cinna, and Metellus discuss whether Cicero should be included in their group, but Brutus objects. Then, Cassius declares that Antony is dangerous and should die along with Caesar. But Brutus argues for restraint assuring him that with Caesar dead, Antony will not be a problem.

CASSIUS. But what of Cicero? Shall we sound him?
    I think he will stand very strong with us.

CASCA. Let us not leave him out.

CINNA.   No, by no means.

METELLUS. O let us have him, for his silver hairs
    Will purchase us a good opinion   145
    And buy men's voices to commend our deeds.
    It shall be said his judgment rul'd our hands.
    Our youths and wildness shall no whit appear,
    But all be buried in his gravity.

BRUTUS. O, name him not! Let us not break with him,   150
    For he will never follow anything
    That other men begin.

CASSIUS.   Then leave him out.

CASCA. Indeed, he is not fit.

DECIUS. Shall no man else be touch'd, but only Caesar?

CASSIUS. Decius, well urg'd. I think it is not meet   155
    Mark Antony, so well belov'd of Caesar,
    Should outlive Caesar. We shall find of him
    A shrewd contriver; and, you know, his means,
    If he improve them, may well stretch so far
    As to annoy us all; which to prevent,   160
    Let Antony and Caesar fall together.

✱ **BRUTUS.** Our course will seem too bloody, Caius Cassius,
    To cut the head off and then hack the limbs,
    Like wrath in death and envy afterwards;
    For Antony is but a limb of Caesar.   165

---

148 shall no whit appear: will not show at all

149 gravity: respectability

150 break with him: disclose our plans to him

❓ Why do the conspirators want Cicero to join their plot? Why does Brutus object?

155 meet: fitting

157 of him: that he is

158 means: resources

159 improve: uses

160 annoy: harm

❓ How many times does Brutus' opinion differ from Cassius' opinion in this scene? How do you think this would affect Cassius? The others?

164 envy: malice

✱ **Tragic Hero** Who is the true tragic hero of *Julius Caesar*—Caesar or Brutus? Many critics believe that Brutus is the play's true tragic hero. Such a hero is typically a virtuous person with some fatal personal flaw. For example, Brutus' republican idealism is not tempered by hard practicality. Here, he rejects the suggestion of killing Mark Antony along with Caesar, out of concern that "Our course will seem too bloody." As things turn out, this is a fatal mistake, for Antony's eloquence will rouse the Roman people against Caesar's killers.

Cassius continues to worry about Antony, but Brutus prevails. The clock strikes three.

Act II   Scene i

Let's be sacrificers, but not butchers, Caius.
We all stand up against the spirit of Caesar,
And in the spirit of men there is no blood.
O, that we then could come by Caesar's spirit   **169 come by:** get a hold of
And not dismember Caesar! But, alas,   170
Caesar must bleed for it. And, gentle friends,   **171 gentle:** noble
Let's kill him boldly, but not wrathfully.
Let's carve him as a dish fit for the gods,
Not hew him as a carcass fit for hounds.   **174 hew:** hack
And let our hearts, as subtle masters do,   175
Stir up their servants to an act of rage,
And after seem to chide 'em. This shall make   **177 chide 'em:** scold them
Our purpose necessary and not envious;   **178 envious:** spiteful or mean-spirited
Which so appearing to the common eyes,   **179 common eyes:** ordinary people
We shall be call'd purgers, not murderers.   180   **180 purgers:** healers who cure their patients by bloodletting
And for Mark Antony, think not of him;   ❓ How does Brutus hope to make Caesar's death acceptable to the commoners?
For he can do no more than Caesar's arm
When Caesar's head is off.

CASSIUS.   Yet I fear him,
For in the ingrafted love he bears to Caesar—   **184 in the ingrafted:** the deeply felt

BRUTUS. Alas, good Cassius, do not think of him.   185
If he love Caesar, all that he can do
Is to himself: take thought and die for Caesar.
And that were much he should, for he is given   **188 were much he should:** would be beyond his ability
To sports, to wildness, and much company.   **189 much company:** enjoyment of his friend's company

TREBONIUS. There is no fear in him. Let him not die,   190   **190 no fear:** nothing to be feared
For he will live and laugh at this hereafter.   ❓ Why do you think Cassius still fears Antony?

✱ *[Clock strikes.]*

✱ **Clock? What Clock?** *"Clock strikes,"* reads a stage direction in this scene. This striking clock is one of the most famous anachronisms in all of Shakespeare. Striking clocks were not invented until the 13th century—well over a thousand years after the death of Julius Caesar.

Cassius wonders if Caesar will actually go to the Capitol. He is known to be superstitious, and the night has been full of bad omens. Decius says that he will make sure that Caesar attends as planned. The group agrees to meet the next morning to accompany Caesar to the Capitol.

BRUTUS. Peace, count the clock.

CASSIUS.   The clock hath stricken three.

TREBONIUS. 'Tis time to part.

CASSIUS.   But it is doubtful yet
  Whether Caesar will come forth today or no,
  For he is superstitious grown of late,   195
  Quite from the main opinion he held once
  Of fantasy, of dreams, and ceremonies.
  It may be these apparent prodigies,
  The unaccustom'd terror of this night,
  And the persuasion of his augurers,   200
  May hold him from the Capitol today.

DECIUS. Never fear that. If he be so resolv'd,
  I can o'ersway him, for he loves to hear
✱ That unicorns may be betray'd with trees,
  And bears with glasses, elephants with holes,   205
  Lions with toils and men with flatterers.
  But when I tell him he hates flatterers,
  He says he does, being then most flatterèd.
  Let me work,
  For I can give his humour the true bent,   210
  And I will bring him to the Capitol.

CASSIUS. Nay, we will all of us be there to fetch him.

BRUTUS. By the eighth hour, is that the uttermost?

CINNA. Be that the uttermost, and fail not then.

195 grown of late: lately

196 from the ... once: opposite from what he used to believe

197 ceremonies: bad omens

198 apparent prodigies: conspicuous omens

200 augurers: fortune-tellers

203 o'ersway: persuade

204 betray'd with trees: trapped by impaling their horns in trees

205 glasses: mirrors; **holes:** pitfalls

206 toils: nets

210 give his ... bent: change his mind

❓ Why does Decius think he can convince Caesar to go to the Capitol?

212 fetch: escort

213 uttermost: latest time

✱ **Animal Traps** The unicorn—a mythical, horse-like creature with a single horn in its forehead—could supposedly be caught by tricking it into ramming its horn into a tree. Mirrors could supposedly be used to catch bears by distracting them with their own reflections.

The conspirators decide to include Caius Ligarius in their plot, and then say goodnight. After the visitors leave, Portia, Brutus' wife, enters.

Act II Scene i

METELLUS. Caius Ligarius doth bear Caesar hard,   215
    Who rated him for speaking well of Pompey.
    I wonder none of you have thought of him.

BRUTUS. Now, good Metellus, go along by him.
    He loves me well, and I have given him reasons.
    Send him but hither, and I'll fashion him.   220

CASSIUS. The morning comes upon's. We'll leave you, Brutus.
    And, friends, disperse yourselves, but all remember
    What you have said, and show yourselves true Romans.

BRUTUS. Good gentlemen, look fresh and merrily.
    Let not our looks put on our purposes,   225
    But bear it, as our Roman actors do,
    With untir'd spirits and formal constancy.
    And so good morrow to you every one.

[Exeunt. BRUTUS *remains.]*

    Boy! Lucius!—Fast asleep? It is no matter.
    Enjoy the honey-heavy dew of slumber.   230
    Thou hast no figures nor no fantasies
    Which busy care draws in the brains of men;
    Therefore thou sleep'st so sound.

[Enter Portia.]

PORTIA.   Brutus, my lord.

BRUTUS. Portia! What mean you? Wherefore rise you now?
    It is not for your health thus to commit   235
    Your weak condition to the raw cold morning.

215 doth bear Caesar hard: resent Caesar

216 rated: scolded

218 by him: to him

220 fashion him: convince him

221 upon's: upon us

PERSONA JOURNAL

Which of the conspirators do you know the best? Explain how you know him and give your opinion of his character.

225 put on: reveal

227 formal constancy: outward composure

230 honey-heavy dew of slumber: deep sleep, heavy like a honeyed dew

231 figures nor no fantasies: images or the troubled dreams

235 for your ... commit: good for your health to expose

Portia is concerned about Brutus. He replies that he has not been feeling well, but Portia doesn't believe him.

✴ **PORTIA.** Nor for yours neither. Y'have ungently, Brutus,
    Stole from my bed. And yesternight at supper
    You suddenly arose and walk'd about,
    Musing and sighing, with your arms across,   240
    And when I ask'd you what the matter was,
    You star'd upon me with ungentle looks.
    I urg'd you further; then you scratch'd your head,
    And too impatiently stamp'd with your foot.
    Yet I insisted; yet you answered not,   245
    But with an angry wafture of your hand
    Gave sign for me to leave you. So I did,
    Fearing to strengthen that impatience
    Which seemed too much enkindled, and withal
    Hoping it was but an effect of humour,   250
    Which sometime hath his hour with every man.
    It will not let you eat nor talk nor sleep,
    And could it work so much upon your shape
    As it hath much prevail'd on your condition,
    I should not know you Brutus. Dear my lord,   255
    Make me acquainted with your cause of grief.

BRUTUS. I am not well in health, and that is all.

PORTIA. Brutus is wise and, were he not in health,
    He would embrace the means to come by it.

BRUTUS. Why, so I do. Good Portia, go to bed.   260

PORTIA. Is Brutus sick? And is it physical
    To walk unbracèd and suck up the humours
    Of the dank morning? What, is Brutus sick,
    And will he steal out of his wholesome bed

---

237 Y'have ungently: You have been discourteous

246 wafture: wave

249 enkindled: inflamed; **withal:** at the same time

250 but an effect of humour: just a passing mood

253 shape: appearance

254 condition: mental state

255 know you: recognize you

259 embrace the … it: take the necessary steps to get better

261 physical: good for your health

262 unbracèd and … humours: around with your jacket unbuttoned and inhale the mists

---

✴ **Double Negatives** Today, we are taught not to use double negatives. According to our rules, Portia really should say, "Nor for yours *either*." But in Shakespeare's time, double negatives were considered perfectly proper, as they are in some other languages (Spanish, for example) today.

✳ To dare the vile contagion of the night   265
  And tempt the rheumy and unpurgèd air
  To add unto his sickness? No, my Brutus,
  You have some sick offense within your mind,
  Which by the right and virtue of my place
  I ought to know of.

[She kneels]

                          And upon my knees,   270
  I charm you, by my once commended beauty,
  By all your vows of love, and that great vow
  Which did incorporate and make us one,
  That you unfold to me, your self, your half,

266 rheumy and unpurgèd: damp and unpurified

271 charm: beg of

273 did incorpoate: brought us together

274 half: other half

Brutus (Martin Sheen) and
Portia (Joan MacIntosh).
New York Shakespeare Festival, 1988.

✳ **"Contagion of the night"** In Shakespeare's time, the night air was believed to be full of disease and infection, and therefore dangerous to one's health. Even so, moody, brooding people like Brutus seemed to find it irresistible to walk outside at night.

Portia inquires about the men who visited Brutus earlier in the evening and continues to urge Brutus to confide in her. A husband should have no secrets from his wife, she insists.

Why you are heavy, and what men tonight   275
Have had resort to you; for here have been
Some six or seven who did hide their faces
Even from darkness.

BRUTUS.   Kneel not, gentle Portia.

[He lifts her up.]

PORTIA. I should not need, if you were gentle Brutus.
Within the bond of marriage, tell me, Brutus,   280
Is it excepted I should know no secrets
That appertain to you? Am I your self
But, as it were, in sort or limitation,
To keep with you at meals, comfort your bed,
And talk to you sometimes? Dwell I but in the suburbs   285
Of your good pleasure? If it be no more,
Portia is Brutus' harlot, not his wife.

BRUTUS. You are my true and honourable wife,
As dear to me as are the ruddy drops
That visit my sad heart.   290

PORTIA. If this were true, then should I know this secret.
I grant I am a woman, but withal
A woman that Lord Brutus took to wife.
I grant I am a woman, but withal
✱ A woman well-reputed, Cato's daughter.   295
Think you I am no stronger than my sex,
Being so father'd and so husbanded?
Tell me your counsels; I will not disclose 'em.
I have made strong proof of my constancy,

275 heavy: depressed

276 had resort to: visited

281 Is it excepted: Is there an exception that

283 in sort or limitation: but with certain conditions and restrictions

289 ruddy drops: blood

PERSONA JOURNAL

What kind of person is Portia? Write about what you know or have heard.

294 withal: also

298 counsels: secrets

299 made strong ... constancy: have proven my strength of character

❓ Do you think that this is a typical Roman husband/wife relationship for the time period?

✱ **Family Matters** Portia is rightly proud to be the daughter of Marcus Porcius Cato (95–46 B.C.), who also happened to be Brutus' uncle. Allied with Pompey, Cato courageously tried to overthrow Caesar. When his army was defeated in northern Africa by Caesar's forces, Cato committed suicide rather than be taken prisoner.

Portia shows Brutus a wound she has made in her thigh in order to prove her fortitude and devotion to him. The couple is interrupted by a knock at the door. Brutus asks Portia to go to another part of the house, promising to tell her everything later. Caius Ligarius enters.

Giving myself a voluntary wound   300
Here, in the thigh. Can I bear that with patience,
And not my husband's secrets?

BRUTUS.   O ye gods!
Render me worthy of this noble wife.

[Knock.]

Hark, hark, one knocks. Portia, go in awhile,
And by and by thy bosom shall partake   305
The secrets of my heart.
✱ All my engagements I will construe to thee,
All the charactery of my sad brows.
Leave me with haste.

[Exit PORTIA.*]*

                    Lucius, who's that knocks?

[Enter LUCIUS *and* LIGARIUS.*]*

LUCIUS. Here is a sick man that would speak with you.   310

BRUTUS. Caius Ligarius, that Metellus spake of.—
    Boy, stand aside.

[Exit LUCIUS.*]*

                    Caius Ligarius, how?

LIGARIUS. Vouchsafe good morrow from a feeble tongue.

BRUTUS. O, what a time have you chose out, brave Caius,
    To wear a kerchief! Would you were not sick!   315

LIGARIUS. I am not sick, if Brutus have in hand
    Any exploit worthy the name of honour.

❓ What do you think about Portia deliberately wounding herself?

305 by and by thy bosom shall partake: very soon you will know

307 engagements: affairs; **construe:** fully explain

308 charactery of: meaning written on

❓ Why do you think that Brutus has not shared his concerns with Portia?

311 spake: spoke

312 how: how are you?

313 Vouchsafe: Please accept

314 chose out: chosen
315 To wear a kerchief: To be ill

❓ What is Ligarius' "sickness"?

✱ **"All my engagements I will construe to thee,"** Brutus says to Portia, promising to tell her about the conspiracy. But he is immediately distracted by Ligarius' entrance. In Scene iv of this act, we'll find out that Portia *has* learned about the conspiracy from her husband.

BRUTUS. Such an exploit have I in hand, Ligarius,
✳ Had you a healthful ear to hear of it.

LIGARIUS. By all the gods that Romans bow before,   320
   I here discard my sickness.

[He takes off his kerchief.]

                              Soul of Rome,
   Brave son deriv'd from honourable loins,
   Thou like an exorcist hast conjur'd up
   My mortifièd spirit. Now bid me run,
   And I will strive with things impossible,   325
   Yea, get the better of them. What's to do?

BRUTUS. A piece of work that will make sick men whole.

LIGARIUS. But are not some whole that we must make sick?

BRUTUS. That must we also. What it is, my Caius,
   I shall unfold to thee as we are going   330
   To whom it must be done.

LIGARIUS.   Set on your foot,
   And with a heart new-fir'd I follow you
   To do I know not what; but it sufficeth
   That Brutus leads me on.

[Thunder.]

BRUTUS.   Follow me then.

[Exeunt.]

322 loins: ancestors

324 mortifièd: deadened

326 What's to do: What do you need me to do?

❓ What does Brutus mean in line 327?

331 Set on your foot: Lead the way

332 new-fir'd: inspired
333 sufficeth: is enough

PERSONA JOURNAL

Describe someone that you would support and follow no matter what.

LOYALTY CHECK

If you wish to change sides, turn over your badge and/or change sides of the classroom.

✳ **Extended Metaphor** As you know, a metaphor is a figure of speech that compares two unlike things without using the words *like* or *as*. An *extended metaphor* is the same type of comparison that goes on for several lines. On this page, Brutus and Ligarius speak metaphorically about sickness and health. Where does the metaphor begin? Where does it end?

Setting the Scene
JULIUS CAESAR

Act II, Scene ii *or* Dream Interpretations

Critical Query: What do Caesar's responses to events in this scene tell you about him?

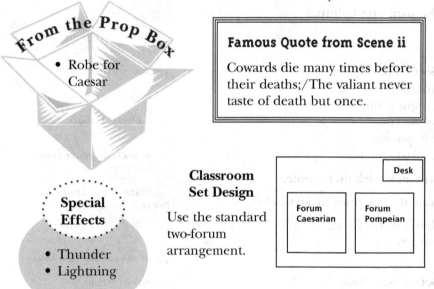

From the Prop Box

- Robe for Caesar

Special Effects

- Thunder
- Lightning

Famous Quote from Scene ii

Cowards die many times before their deaths;/The valiant never taste of death but once.

Classroom Set Design

Use the standard two-forum arrangement.

Desk

Forum Caesarian

Forum Pompeian

In Character: Chatting with Caesar

At the end of this scene you'll have a chance to find out more about Caesar. The actor(s) who played him must sit in the hot seat and answer questions in character. Feel free to ask him how he feels about other characters, what he thinks the future will hold, what will happen if Calpurnia doesn't bear an heir, and so forth.

Time Capsule: Augury

"What say the augurers?" asks Caesar (page 78), who wants to know if the day will be favorable. Augury was a method of predicting the future that was practiced in many ancient civilizations. In Caesar's time such fortune-tellers were special priests paid by the government. Shakespeare misused the term *augury* since this referred specifically to telling the future by interpreting the sounds and flight patterns of birds. *Haruspicy* refers to reading the entrails of animals, preferably sheep. Those that practiced this form of divination were known as *haruspices*.

Warm-Up Improv 1	Warm-Up Improv 2
You are planning a vacation with your family, but the night before you are supposed to leave, your mother has a bad dream that convinces her the trip should be postponed. You and the rest of the family try to change her mind.	An *aside* is a speech or comment spoken directly to the audience so that the other characters on stage can't hear. Repeat Improv 1 with all characters using asides to show their true feelings.

Caesar is at home in his dressing gown pondering the meaning of the night's strange omens. Calpurnia, Caesar's wife, enters and begs him not to go out. She is frightened by a bad dream and the abnormal events that have occurred.

Scene ii: Rome. Caesar's House

[Thunder and lightning. Enter JULIUS CAESAR *in his nightgown.]*

✱ **CAESAR.** Nor heaven nor earth have been at peace tonight.
  Thrice has Calpurnia in her sleep cried out,
  "Help ho, they murder Caesar!"—Who's within?

[Enter a SERVANT.*]*

SERVANT. My lord.

CAESAR. Go bid the priests do present sacrifice,   5
  And bring me their opinions of success.

SERVANT. I will, my lord.

[Exit SERVANT.*]*

[Enter CALPURNIA.*]*

CALPURNIA. What mean you, Caesar? Think you to walk forth?
  You shall not stir out of your house today.

CAESAR. Caesar shall forth; the things that threatened me   10
  Ne'er looked but on my back. When they shall see
  The face of Caesar, they are vanishèd.

CALPURNIA. Caesar, I never stood on ceremonies,
  Yet now they fright me. There is one within,
  Besides the things that we have heard and seen,   15
  Recounts most horrid sights seen by the watch.
  A lioness hath whelpèd in the streets,
  And graves have yawn'd and yielded up their dead.
  Fierce fiery warriors fought upon the clouds
  In ranks and squadrons and right form of war,   20

nightgown: dressing gown

1 Nor Heaven nor: Neither heaven nor

PERSONA JOURNAL

Describe your household's reactions to the events of the night.

3 within: on duty inside

5 bid: tell; **do present sacrifice:** to immediately sacrifice an animal (Roman priests examined the inner organs of sacrificed animals to predict the future.)

13 stood on ceremonies: believed in omens

14 one within: someone inside

16 Recounts: Who tells about; **watch:** watchmen

17 whelpèd: given birth

18 yawn'd: opened

20 right form: proper order

PERSONA JOURNAL

Do you believe in omens and fortune-tellers?

✱ **It Was a Dark and Stormy Night ...** Soon after Shakespeare wrote *Julius Caesar*, he wrote *Hamlet*, which contains some fascinating echoes of the earlier play. For example, compare Calpurnia's description of the stormy night to Horatio's lines from *Hamlet* (Act I, Scene i):

A little ere the mightiest Julius fell,/The graves stood tenantless, and the sheeted dead
Did squeak and gibber in the Roman streets—/As stars with trains of fire and dews of blood ...

Caesar is curious about Calpurnia's dream and the night's strange events, but he does not fear them. He believes that death lies in the hands of the gods. Even after Caesar is told that the fortune-tellers have also warned him not to leave the house, Caesar insists that he is not afraid.

Which drizzled blood upon the Capitol.
The noise of battle hurtl'd in the air,
Horses did neigh, and dying men did groan,
And ghosts did shriek and squeal about the streets.
O Caesar, these things are beyond all use,   25
And I do fear them.

CAESAR.   What can be avoided
Whose end is purpos'd by the mighty gods?
Yet Caesar shall go forth, for these predictions
Are to the world in general as to Caesar.

* **CALPURNIA.** When beggars die, there are no comets seen;   30
The heavens themselves blaze forth the death of princes.

CAESAR. Cowards die many times before their deaths;
The valiant never taste of death but once.
Of all the wonders that I yet have heard,
It seems to me most strange that men should fear,   35
Seeing that death, a necessary end,
Will come when it will come.

[Enter a SERVANT.]

                What say the augurers?

SERVANT. They would not have you to stir forth today.
Plucking the entrails of an offering forth,
They could not find a heart within the beast.   40

CAESAR. The gods do this in shame of cowardice.
Caesar should be a beast without a heart
If he should stay at home today for fear.

22 hurtl'd: clashed

25 beyond all use: strange and abnormal

28 Yet: Even so
29 Are to: Apply

31 blaze forth: announce

❓ What is Caesar's attitude about death?

37 augurers: fortune-tellers

39 an offering: a sacrificed animal

41 in shame of cowardice: to put cowards to shame

* **Doubling** An eye-witness to the original 1599 production of *Julius Caesar*, Thomas Platter, described the performance in his journal. He estimated that the play was performed by about 15 actors. This is interesting—considering that the play contains more than 40 speaking parts. Several actors must have played more than one role to make this possible—a practice called *doubling*. Some scholars have suggested that Portia and Calpurnia may have been played by the same boy actor.

Caesar declares that he will go out but Calpurnia pleads with him to reconsider. He finally gives in to her wishes. Decius arrives, and Caesar orders him to tell the Senate that he will not attend. Calpurnia suggests that Decius say Caesar is sick.

No, Caesar shall not. Danger knows full well
That Caesar is more dangerous than he.   45
We are two lions litter'd in one day,
And I the elder and more terrible.
And Caesar shall go forth.

CALPURNIA.   Alas, my lord,
Your wisdom is consum'd in confidence.
Do not go forth today. Call it my fear   50
That keeps you in the house, and not your own.
We'll send Mark Antony to the Senate House,
And he shall say you are not well today.
Let me upon my knee prevail in this.

[She kneels.]

CAESAR. Mark Antony shall say I am not well,   55
And for thy humour I will stay at home.

[He lifts her up.]

[Enter Decius.]

Here's Decius Brutus, he shall tell them so.

DECIUS. Caesar, all hail! Good morrow, worthy Caesar;
I come to fetch you to the Senate House.

CAESAR. And you are come in very happy time   60
To bear my greeting to the senators
And tell them that I will not come today.
Cannot is false and that I dare not, falser.
I will not come today. Tell them so, Decius.

CALPURNIA. Say he is sick.

46 litter'd: born

? How might Calpurnia play this scene in order to convince Caesar to stay at home?

56 humour: mood

59 fetch: escort

60 in very happy time: at the right moment

63 falser: falsify

? How does the relationship between Caesar and Calpurnia seem different from that of Brutus and Portia?

Caesar becomes cross with Calpurnia for instructing Decius to lie for him. He haughtily instructs Decius to simply say that he will not come. Decius asks for a reason to give the Senate. Caesar replies that his word is reason enough for the Senate; however, he privately tells Decius about Calpurnia's concerns.

Act II   Scene ii

CAESAR.   Shall Caesar send a lie?   65
     Have I in conquest stretch'd mine arm so far,
     To be afeared to tell graybeards the truth?
     Decius, go tell them Caesar will not come.

DECIUS. Most mighty Caesar, let me know some cause,
     Lest I be laugh'd at when I tell them so.   70

CAESAR. The cause is in my will. I will not come.
     That is enough to satisfy the Senate.
     But for your private satisfaction,
     Because I love you, I will let you know.
     Calpurnia here, my wife, stays me at home.   75   **75 stays:** keeps

Calpurnia (Judy Parfitt) begs Caesar (John Gielgud) not to go to the Senate. Commonwealth United film directed by Stuart Burge, 1970.

80

Decius interprets Calpurnia's dreams differently and convinces Caesar to reconsider. He goes on to tell Caesar that the Senate has decided to crown him king on this very day.

✱ She dreamt tonight she saw my statue,
Which, like a fountain with an hundred spouts
Did run pure blood; and many lusty Romans
Came smiling and did bathe their hands in it.
And these does she apply for warnings and portents   80
And evils imminent, and on her knee
Hath begg'd that I will stay at home today.

DECIUS. This dream is all amiss interpreted.
It was a vision fair and fortunate.
Your statue spouting blood in many pipes,   85
In which so many smiling Romans bath'd,
Signifies that from you great Rome shall suck
Reviving blood, and that great men shall press
For tinctures, stains, relics, and cognizance.
This by Calpurnia's dream is signified.   90

CAESAR. And this way have you well expounded it.

DECIUS. I have, when you have heard what I can say.
And know it now: the Senate have concluded
To give this day a crown to mighty Caesar.
If you shall send them word you will not come,   95
Their minds may change. Besides, it were a mock
Apt to be render'd, for someone to say,
"Break up the Senate till another time,
When Caesar's wife shall meet with better dreams."
If Caesar hide himself, shall they not whisper.   100
"Lo, Caesar is afraid"?
Pardon me, Caesar, for my dear dear love
To your proceeding bids me tell you this,
And reason to my love is liable.

78 lusty: merry

80 apply: interpret; **portents:** bad omens

88–89 press/For ... cognizance: be eager to possess handkerchiefs stained with your blood, holy souvenirs and emblems to be worn to show they are your followers

91 this way ... it: your explanation is convincing

❓ Do you think that the Senate really intends to crown Caesar king today?

96–97 it were ... say: it would be an opportunity for someone to easily insult you by saying

103 To your proceeding: For your advancement

104 reason to ... liable: because I love you so, I have dared to speak so freely

❓ What arguments does Decius use to manipulate Caesar into going to the Capitol?

✱ **Broken and Bloody** Although Shakespeare drew many details of *Julius Caesar* from the Greek historian Plutarch's *Lives*, he didn't shy away from changing Plutarch for his own dramatic purposes. For example, according to Plutarch, Calpurnia dreamed that an ornament atop Caesar's house fell down and broke, "and that she thought she lamented and wept for it." Shakespeare changed this to a dream of Caesar's statue spouting fountains of blood—certainly a more powerful image.

Admonishing Calpurnia for her fears, Caesar changes his mind, declaring that he will go to the Capitol after all. The group of conspirators arrives, along with Antony, to accompany Caesar to the Senate.

CAESAR. How foolish do your fears seem now, Calpurnia! 105
    I am ashamèd I did yield to them.
    Give me my robe, for I will go.

[Enter BRUTUS, LIGARIUS, METELLUS, CASCA, TREBONIUS, CINNA, *and* PUBLIUS.*]*

    And look where Publius is come to fetch me.

PUBLIUS. Good morrow, Caesar.

CAESAR.   Welcome, Publius.—
    What, Brutus, are you stirr'd so early too?— 110
    Good morrow, Casca.—Caius Ligarius,
    Caesar was ne'er so much your enemy
    As that same ague which hath made you lean.—
    What is't o'clock?

BRUTUS.   Caesar, 'tis stricken eight.

CAESAR. I thank you for your pains and courtesy. 115

[Enter Antony.]

✴ See, Antony that revels long a-nights
    Is notwithstanding up.—Good morrow, Antony.

? How has Calpurnia been reacting as Decius works at changing Caesar's mind?

112 enemy: Ligarius had recently been pardoned by Caesar. Ligarius had supported Pompey against Caesar in the civil war.

113 ague: fever

116–117 that revels ... up: who stays out late partying is also up

Frank Benson as Mark Antony

✴ **Party on, Mark!** Caesar is surprised to see Antony up and around so early. And indeed, Antony is probably a bit hungover, for he really did love to drink and party. This reckless, fun-loving aspect of Antony's personality is more fully portrayed in Shakespeare's later tragedy, *Antony and Cleopatra.*

ANTONY. So to most noble Caesar.

CAESAR.   Bid them prepare within.
I am to blame to be thus waited for.
Now Cinna.—Now Metellus. What, Trebonius,   120
I have an hour's talk in store for you.
Remember that you call on me today;
Be near me that I may remember you.

TREBONIUS. Caesar, I will. *[Aside]* And so near will I be,
That your best friends shall wish I had been further.   125

CAESAR. Good friends, go in and taste some wine with me,
And we, like friends, will straightway go together.

BRUTUS. *[Aside]* That every like is not the same, O Caesar,
 ✱ The heart of Brutus earns to think upon.

[Exeunt.]

118 them: the servants; **prepare:** refers to wine

122 Remember that ... today: Remind me to speak to you today

127 straightway: soon

❓ What is ironic about Caesar's speech in lines 126–127?

128 That every ... same: Referring back to Caesar's reference to "like friends," Brutus responds with an altered version of the Latin proverb *Omne simile non est idem* or "All that is alike is not the same."

129 earns: grieves

LOYALTY CHECK
Will you switch or stay as you are?

✱ **Tragic Hero, Revisited** If, as many critics believe, Brutus is the hero of *Julius Caesar*, why isn't the play named after him? Like Brutus, Caesar has many characteristics of a tragic hero. His virtues include bravery, intelligence, and courtesy; his flaws include vanity, superstition, power lust, and a weakness for flattery. Perhaps some critics discount Caesar as the play's tragic hero simply because of the size of his part. He has only the play's fourth-largest role, while Brutus has by far the greatest number of lines.

Setting the Scene

JULIUS CAESAR

Act II, Scenes iii and iv *or* The Tension Grows

Critical Query: What is the purpose of these two brief scenes?

Classroom Set Design

Use the standard two-forum design. Artemidorus reads as he walks up the center aisle toward the playing area. He exits stage left. Portia and Lucius enter and play their scene upstage right. For future reference, learn the following stage terminology: **upstage** means away from the audience and **downstage** means toward or closer to the audience. **Stage left** and **stage right** refer to the *actor's* left and right as he/she faces the audience.

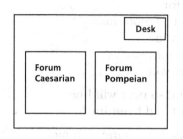

Desk

Forum Caesarian

Forum Pompeian

From the Prop Box

- Letter written by Artemidorus

Time Capsule: The Fates

In Scene iii, Artemidorus tries to warn Caesar with a note: "If thou read this, O Caesar, thou mayest live;/If not, the Fates with traitors do contrive." His reference to the Fates touches a theme found in many of Shakespeare's plays — our destinies are not in our hands but rather dictated by a divine plan. In Caesar's time the Fates were three sister goddesses who wove the tapestry of each life. Clotho combed the wool and spun the thread of life; Lachesis measured it; and Atropos cut it with her scissors.

Who's Who? Artemidorus

As you will learn in the next scene, one minor character has discovered the assassination plot. Artemidorus was a Doctor of Rhetoric, or in other words, a speech teacher. Skillful oratory was a necessary quality for a successful career, and Artemidorus had apparently been coaching several of the conspirators who let details of the plan slip out.

Warm-Up Improv 1

Someone you know is in danger. Make a call and try to warn him/her. Remember that during an on-stage phone conversation, you must stop and "listen" to the other party.

Warm-Up Improv 2

The car you're riding in has run into a ditch and the driver's hurt. You are panicked and race back and forth between the road where you hope to flag someone down and the driver, whom you are trying to keep calm.

Out on the street, Artemidorus, a friend of Caesar's, reads a note he has written to warn Caesar about impending danger. He plans to present it as Caesar passes by.

Scene iii. Rome. A Street

Enter ARTEMIDORUS, *reading a paper.]*

ARTEMIDORUS. "Caesar, beware of Brutus, take heed of
    Cassius, come not near Casca, have an eye to Cinna,
    trust not Trebonius, mark well Metellus Cimber,
    Decius Brutus loves thee not. Thou hast wronged
    Caius Ligarius. There is but one mind in all these   5
    men, and it is bent against Caesar. If thou beest
    not immortal, look about you. Security gives way
    to conspiracy. The mighty gods defend thee!
    Thy lover, Artemidorus."
    Here will I stand till Caesar pass along,   10
    And as a suitor will I give him this.
    My heart laments that virtue cannot live
    Out of the teeth of emulation.
    If thou read this, O Caesar, thou mayest live;
    If not, the Fates with traitors do contrive.

[Exit ARTEMIDORUS.]

❓ Do you think Artemidorus knows about the plot to kill Caesar or does he just suspect it?

7 Security: Overconfidence

9 lover: friend

11 suitor: petitioner

13 teeth of emulation: reach of envy

15 Fates: The goddesses who ruled the lives of men; **contrive:** plot

PERSONA JOURNAL

You are preparing to petition Caesar for a favor as well. What is the favor?

At Brutus' house, an agitated Portia orders Lucius to run to the Senate to see if Brutus is well.

Act II   Scene iv

Scene iv: Rome. Before the House of Brutus

[Enter PORTIA *and* LUCIUS.*]*

PORTIA. I prithee, boy, run to the Senate House;
Stay not to answer me, but get thee gone.
✱ Why dost thou stay?

LUCIUS.   To know my errand, madam.

PORTIA. I would have had thee there and here again
Ere I can tell thee what thou shouldst do there.   5
[Aside] O constancy, be strong upon my side;
Set a huge mountain 'tween my heart and tongue.
I have a man's mind but a woman's might.
How hard it is for women to keep counsel!—
Art thou here yet?

LUCIUS.   Madam, what should I do?   10
Run to the Capitol, and nothing else?
And so return to you, and nothing else?

PORTIA. Yes, bring me word, boy, if thy lord look well,
For he went sickly forth. And take good note
What Caesar doth, what suitors press to him.   15
Hark, boy, what noise is that?

LUCIUS. I hear none, madam.

PORTIA.   Prithee listen well.
I heard a bustling rumour like a fray,
And the wind brings it from the Capitol.

LUCIUS. Sooth, madam, I hear nothing.   20

1 prithee: pray thee

5 Ere: Before

6 constancy: self-control

8 might: strength
9 counsel: a secret

❓ Portia seems anxious and nervous. Do you think she knows about the plot against Caesar? Why or why not?

15 press to: crowd around

18 bustling rumour like a fray: confused noise like a street fight

20 Sooth: Truly

✱ **Thou and Thee** By this point in the play, you're probably comfortable with Shakespeare's use of "thou" and "thee." But have you noticed that he uses "you" more often than he does these old-fashioned words? By Shakespeare's time, "thou" and "thee" were starting to disappear from the language.

Before he can leave, a soothsayer approaches and Portia nervously asks him for any news about Caesar. The soothsayer confides that he plans to warn Caesar about possible danger.

✱ [*Enter the* SOOTHSAYER.]

PORTIA. Come hither, fellow. Which way hast thou been?

SOOTHSAYER. At mine own house, good lady.

PORTIA. What is't o'clock?

SOOTHSAYER.   About the ninth hour, lady.

PORTIA. Is Caesar yet gone to the Capitol?

SOOTHSAYER. Madam, not yet. I go to take my stand,   25
    To see him pass on to the Capitol.

Soothsayer: the same fortune-teller who warned Caesar to beware the ides of March

21 hither: here

23 is't o'clock: time is it

Portia (Lisa Carter) and the Soothsayer (Jessica Perlmeter).
Aquilla Theatre, 2000.

✱ **Blind Prophet?** For some reason, the soothsayer is portrayed as blind in almost all productions of *Julius Caesar*—even though neither Shakespeare nor Plutarch suggests that he is blind. Perhaps directors and actors think of him as resembling Tiresias—the prophet of Greek mythology who really *was* blind and who appeared in ancient Greek tragedies such as Sophocles' *Oedipus the King* and *Antigone*.

Portia sends Lucius to the Capitol with a message of support for her husband and instructs Lucius to bring her a reply.

Act II   Scene iv

PORTIA. Thou hast some suit to Caesar, hast thou not?

SOOTHSAYER. That I have, lady. If it will please Caesar
    To be so good to Caesar as to hear me,
    I shall beseech him to befriend himself.   30

PORTIA. Why, know'st thou any harm's intended towards him?

SOOTHSAYER. None that I know will be, much that I fear may chance.
    Good morrow to you. Here the street is narrow.
    The throng that follows Caesar at the heels,
    Of senators, of praetors, common suitors,   35
    Will crowd a feeble man almost to death.
    I'll get me to a place more void, and there
    Speak to great Caesar as he comes along.

[Exit the SOOTHSAYER.*]*

PORTIA. I must go in. *[Aside]* Ay me, how weak a thing
    The heart of woman is! O Brutus,   40
    The heavens speed thee in thine enterprise!
    Sure the boy heard me. *[To* LUCIUS.*]* Brutus hath a suit
    That Caesar will not grant. *[Aside.]* O I grow faint.—
✱ Run, Lucius, and commend me to my lord.
    Say I am merry. Come to me again   45
    And bring me word what he doth say to thee.

[Exeunt at different doors.]

27 suit to: request of

PERSONA JOURNAL

You see Caesar as he walks to the Capitol. Describe the sight.

35 praetors: magistrates

37 place more void: more open area

42 Sure: Surely

44 commend me: give my regards

45 merry: joyful

✱ **Where Are We?** In this scene, Portia sends Lucius to the Senate House at the Capitol. If he had tried to follow these directions he would have never seen Brutus! The Senate House was not at the Capitol. It was one of the buildings facing the Roman Forum. The Forum was a meeting and marketplace surrounded by government buildings, theatres, temples, and so on. The Capitol was actually a great national temple dedicated to Jupiter that sat high on a hill overlooking the Forum. It had nothing to do with the Senate.

Joseph Holland as Caesar is assassinated by Brutus (Orson Welles) and Cassius (Martin Gabel). Mitcheson and Mander Collection.

Antony (George Coulouris), in the costume of a dictator, speaks to the citizens below. Billy Rose Theatre Collection, NY Public Library at Lincoln Center

Orson Welles as Brutus. Museum of the City of New York.

TALES FROM THE STAGE
A Reflection of the Times

During the 1930s, Fascist tyranny was growing in Europe, and ruthless dictators such as Adolf Hitler, Benito Mussolini, and Francisco Franco seized power. In 1937, the young actor/director Orson Welles and his producing partner John Houseman staged a New York production of *Julius Caesar* that reflected recent political events. Caesar and his followers wore the uniforms of Fascist leaders, while lower-ranking characters wore modern-day street clothes. Welles himself played Brutus in a modest pinstriped suit. The set was minimal, with severe spotlights suggesting a Nazi rally.

The production received almost unanimous rave reviews. It remains legendary for demonstrating the political timelessness of Shakespeare's play.

During early rehearsals, the actors were upset to find that the set was full of open trapdoors. Since many scene changes took place in total darkness, cast members were justifiably concerned about falling into them. When they complained to Welles, the actor/director was indignant. He told them sternly that trapdoors were among the oldest of stage devices. Surely professional actors could find their way around the stage without falling into them!

All seemed to be going well at the play's first dress rehearsal—until the assassination scene. The actor playing Brutus—Welles himself—didn't make his entrance. Actors and crew searched high and low for him. At last, they found that Welles had fallen 15 feet through a trapdoor and been knocked unconscious.

Reacting to Act II

Analysis

1. When Brutus says of Caesar, "I know no personal cause to spurn at him (page 59)," and claims to be reluctant to kill him, how do we know that he is sincere?

2. Do you see any flaws or weaknesses in the conspirators' plans? Think about whether they have overlooked or underestimated anything as well as what the strengths of their plans might be. Explain your opinions.

3. Do you think the conspirators should have chosen someone other than Brutus to be their leader? Who might they have chosen instead?

4. In Scene ii, Caesar says, "Cowards die many times before their deaths;/The valiant never taste of death but once." Explain what you think this famous line means, and then discuss the truth of the statement.

5. At the end of Act II, do you think Caesar has any inkling of his impending fate? Explain.

6. Many people warn Caesar against going to the Capitol on March 15. What do you think is the main reason Caesar decides to go despite all the warnings? Use evidence from both Acts I and II to support your response.

Literary Elements

1. In a **soliloquy** (a speech to himself) on pages 59–61, Brutus states his doubts about attacking Caesar. What does Brutus consider good reasons for killing him? You may have more than one answer.

2. **Irony** is a contrast between what appears to be and what actually is. In Scene i, Decius says, "But when I tell [Caesar] he hates flatterers,/He says he does, being then most flatterèd." Explain the irony.

3. A **theme** is an author's ongoing topic, idea, or concern. The theme of sickness runs throughout Act II. Name some of the ways in which this idea is used. What point do you think Shakespeare makes by continually referring to this theme?

Writing

1. In Act II, scene i, Metellus urges the other conspirators to bring Cicero on board in order to help "purchase us a good opinion/and buy men's voices to commend our deeds." Brutus worries that killing Antony would make their "course . . . seem too bloody." At this stage of the conspiracy, what do you think a modern public relations firm would advise these men? Write out a plan that would maximize public approval of the revolt against Caesar and minimize public fallout. Include any special events you might plan, posters or flyers, public gifts or allowances, and so forth that would help your clients— the conspirators—prevail with confidence.

2. In Scene i, Brutus receives a mysterious letter that urges him to rise up against Caesar. Write a different version of this conspiratorial letter, one that uses facts and reasons instead of strange and emotional appeals. Why do you think Cassius chooses the latter form of communication to appeal to Brutus?

3. Julius Caesar is swayed by pressure from others in Act II, Scene ii. Write about a time someone influenced you. Explain how this person convinced you to act or think a certain way.

Julius Caesar Act III

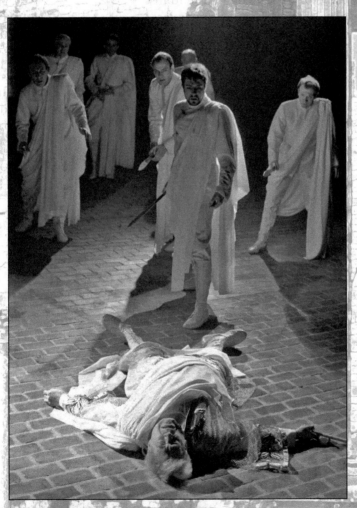

The conspirators with Caesar's body. The Royal Shakespeare Company, Stratford-on-Avon, 1987.

"Liberty! Freedom! Tyranny is dead!"

Setting the Scene

JULIUS CAESAR

Act III, Scene i *or* Murder and Mayhem

Critical Query: How will the plot unfold?

Behind the Scene: The Pulpit

When Antony speaks of going to the pulpit to speak at Caesar's funeral, he is referring to the *Rostra* or speakers' platform that was located at the west end of the Roman Forum. The platform was decorated with the prows or *rostra* of captured warships. Our word *rostrum* or "speaking podium" comes from this Latin term.

Literary Lore: Murder by the Book

Shakespeare stays quite true to his source, Plutarch, as he dramatizes Caesar's murder. Plutarch reports that Caesar tried to fend off the first strikes, grabbing the wrist of one assassin and running here and there trying to avoid other blows. However, when he "sawe Brutus with a sworde drawen in his hande readie to strike at him: then he let Cascaes hande goe, and casting his gowne over his face, suffered everie man to strike at him that woulde."

Famous Quotes from Scene i

- I am as constant as the Northern Star. . .
- *Et tu, Brute?*
- How many ages hence shall this our lofty scene be acted over, in states unborn and accents yet unknown!
- Cry "Havoc!" and let slip the dogs of war. . .

Classroom Set Design

Use the basic two-forum design but with student desks pushed back as far as possible to create a larger playing area. Caesar and attendants enter from the center aisle and play the first few lines there. Moving further upstage will indicate that they have entered the Capitol building.

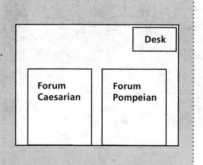

Desk

Forum Caesarian

Forum Pompeian

From the Prop Box

- Paper carried by the Soothsayer
- Daggers for the conspirators

Special Effects

- Trumpet flourish

Warm-Up Improv

You are on a reality TV show. Your closest friend may be the next person voted out of the group. Stand and give an impassioned speech to convince others that this would be a huge mistake.

As Caesar arrives at the Capitol, Artemidorus tries to warn him of impending danger. But Caesar pays no attention.

Act III Scene i

ACT III

Scene i. Rome. Before the Capitol

[Flourish. Enter CAESAR, BRUTUS, CASSIUS, CASCA, DECIUS, METEL-LUS, TREBONIUS, CINNA, ANTONY, LEPIDUS, ARTEMIDORUS, PUBLIUS, POPILIUS, *and the* SOOTHSAYER.*]*

CAESAR. The ides of March are come.

SOOTHSAYER. Ay, Caesar, but not gone.

ARTEMIDORUS. Hail, Caesar. Read this schedule.

DECIUS. Trebonius doth desire you to o'er-read,
    At your best leisure, this his humble suit.   5

ARTEMIDORUS. O Caesar, read mine first, for mine's a suit
    That touches Caesar nearer. Read it, great Caesar.

CAESAR. What touches us ourself shall be last serv'd.

ARTEMIDORUS. Delay not, Caesar; read it instantly.

CAESAR. What, is the fellow mad?

PUBLIUS.   Sirrah, give place.   10

CASSIUS. What, urge you your petitions in the street?
 ✱ Come to the Capitol.

[CAESAR enters the Capitol, the rest following.]

POPILIUS. I wish your enterprise today may thrive.

CASSIUS. What enterprise, Popilius?

PERSONA ACTION

One-fourth of the citizens from each forum trail in with Caesar and his followers. They scatter around the playing area and react in pantomime to the other actors.

❓ What tone might Caesar use for line 1?

3 schedule: note

4 o'er-read: look over or read

5 suit: request

7 touches Caesar nearer: concerns Caesar personally

10 Sirrah, give place: Fellow, get out of the way.

❓ How might Artemidorus react when he is told to move out of the way?

✱ **"Come to the Capitol,"** Cassius tells his fellow senators. But according to Shakespeare's historical source, Plutarch's *Lives*, neither the senate meeting nor Caesar's assassination took place at the Capitol, but instead at Pompey's Theatre (see the note on page 88). Shakespeare apparently didn't know that the Roman Senate building was undergoing repair at the time of Caesar's death.

Brutus and Cassius worry that Popilius has discovered their plans. They see him speaking to Caesar, but it soon appears that their fears are unfounded.

Caesar and senators proceed to the Capitol. Stratford-on-Avon, 1987

POPILIUS.   Fare you well.

[Advances to CAESAR.*]*

BRUTUS. What said Popilius Lena?   15

CASSIUS. He wished today our enterprise might thrive.
  I fear our purpose is discoverèd.

BRUTUS. Look how he makes to Caesar. Mark him.

CASSIUS. Casca, be sudden, for we fear prevention.—
  Brutus, what shall be done? If this be known,   20
  Cassius or Caesar never shall turn back,
  For I will slay myself.

BRUTUS.   Cassius, be constant.
  Popilius Lena speaks not of our purposes,
  For look, he smiles, and Caesar doth not change.

CASSIUS. Trebonius knows his time, for look you, Brutus,   25
  He draws Mark Antony out of the way.

[Exeunt ANTONY *and* TREBONIUS.*]*

---

18 makes to: makes his way to or approaches
19 sudden: quick; **prevention:** that someone will stop us
21 turn back: return home alone
22 constant: strong

? What do you think would have happened if Popilius had told Caesar of the conspirators' plans?

24 Caesar: Caesar's face

? How does Trebonius get Antony away from Caesar? What do you think is said between them?

94

Caesar signals for the Senate proceedings to begin. Metellus seeks clemency for his banished brother. He kneels and praises Ceasar who quickly silences him by declaring that his opinions cannot be swayed by flattery.

DECIUS. Where is Metellus Cimber? Let him go
  And presently prefer his suit to Caesar.

BRUTUS. He is addressed. Press near and second him.

CINNA. Casca, you are the first that rears your hand.   30

CAESAR. Are we all ready? What is now amiss
  That Caesar and his Senate must redress?

METELLUS.

[Kneeling.]

  Most high, most mighty, and most puissant Caesar,
  Metellus Cimber throws before thy seat
  An humble heart.

CAESAR.   I must prevent thee, Cimber.   35
  These couchings and these lowly courtesies
  Might fire the blood of ordinary men
  And turn preordinance and first decree
  Into the law of children. Be not fond
  To think that Caesar bears such rebel blood   40
  That will be thaw'd from the true quality
  With that which melteth fools—I mean sweet words,
  Low-crookèd curtsies, and base spaniel fawning.
  Thy brother by decree is banishèd.
  If thou dost bend and pray and fawn for him,   45
  I spurn thee like a cur out of my way.
  ✳ Know: Caesar doth not wrong, nor without cause
  Will he be satisfied.

METELLUS. Is there no voice more worthy than my own
  To sound more sweetly in great Caesar's ear   50
  For the repealing of my banished brother?

---

28 presently prefer his suit: present his request

29 addressed: ready; **Press near and second him:** Stay close to him and back him up.

30 are the ... hand: will be the first to strike

31 amiss: wrong

32 redress: correct

PERSONA JOURNAL

A second group of personas arrives at the Capitol.

35 prevent thee: stop you

36 couchings: bowings

38–39 turn preordinance ... children: turn what has been ordained and decreed into a childish set of rules; **fond:** foolish

40 rebel blood: an unstable nature

41 thaw'd from the true quality: swayed from its true purpose

42 melteth: moves; **sweet words:** flattery

43 Low-crookèd curtsies ... fawning: Exaggerated bows and the slobbering affection of a spaniel

46 spurn: will kick; **cur:** dog

47 doth not wrong: doesn't commit errors

48 be satisfied: seek prosecution

❓ Do you think Metellus is really concerned about his brother? Why or why not?

51 repealing: recalling

✳ **Peer Editing** Caesar says that he "doth not wrong, nor without cause/Will he be satisfied." But according to Shakespeare's friend and fellow-playwright Ben Jonson, this line originally read something like, "Caesar did never wrong but with just cause,/Nor without cause will he be satisfied." Jonson found this line unintentionally funny. After all, isn't Caesar saying that he never did wrong except when it was right? Shakespeare may have taken Jonson's criticism to heart and revised this line to make it sound less silly.

BRUTUS.

[Kneeling.]

    I kiss thy hand, but not in flattery, Caesar,
    Desiring thee that Publius Cimber may
    Have an immediate freedom of repeal.

CAESAR. What, Brutus?

CASSIUS.

[Kneeling.]

               Pardon, Caesar; Caesar, pardon!   55
    As low as to thy foot doth Cassius fall
    To beg enfranchisement for Publius Cimber.

CAESAR. I could be well mov'd, if I were as you.
    If I could pray to move, prayers would move me.
    But I am constant as the Northern Star,   60

PERSONA JOURNAL

You have heard about the banishment of Publius Cimber. Why was he banished? Explain.

54 freedom of repeal: recall from exile

57 enfranchisement: a reprieve

58 well mov'd: persuaded

59 to move: to persuade others

Cassius, Cinna, and Brutus petition Caesar for a favor. Mankiewicz film, 1953.

Caesar refuses to reconsider the banishment of Metellus' brother. He boasts of his firm and consistent handling of the law, comparing himself to Olympus, the home of the gods. Cinna and Decius start to voice their support for Metellus' brother when Casca suddenly stabs Caesar from behind. The other conspirators quickly follow suit.

❋ Of whose true fix'd and resting quality
There is no fellow in the firmament.
The skies are painted with unnumber'd sparks;
They are all fire, and every one doth shine.
But there's but one in all doth hold his place.   65
So in the world: 'tis furnish'd well with men,
And men are flesh and blood, and apprehensive.
Yet in the number I do know but one
That unassailable holds on his rank,
Unshak'd of motion; and that I am he   70
Let me a little show it, even in this:
That I was constant Cimber should be banish'd,
And constant do remain to keep him so.

CINNA.

[Kneeling.]

O Caesar—

CAESAR.   Hence! Wilt thou lift up Olympus?

DECIUS.

[Kneeling.]

Great Caesar—

CAESAR.   Doth not Brutus bootless kneel?   75

CASCA. Speak, hands, for me!

[As CASCA *strikes, the others rise up and stab* CAESAR.*]*

PERSONA ACTION

Another small group of personas arrives.

62 fellow in the firmament: equal in the heavens

63 unnumber'd: innumerable

66 'tis furnish'd well: it is well stocked

67 apprehensive: capable of reasoning

69–70 That unassailable … motion: Who cannot be tempted and holds his position, unmoved by any influences

72 constant: firm

73 constant do remain: remain firm

❓ Do you think the other senators see anything suspicious about the behavior of the conspirators as they ask Caesar to pardon Publius Cimber?

74 Wilt thou lift up Olympus: Will you try to do the impossible? (Olympus is a mountain in Greece. In mythology, it was thought to be the home of the gods.)

75 bootless kneel: kneel in vain

❓ What opinion would you have of Caesar if you heard him give this speech?

❋ **Irony** *Dramatic irony* is when the audience has important information that characters in the story do not have. *Situational irony* is when the outcome of a situation is the opposite of someone's expectations. In the moments before Caesar's death, Shakespeare brilliantly combines both of these kinds of irony. Comparing himself to the Northern Star and declaring himself almost a god, Caesar has no idea (as we do) that he is about to die. What emotional effect does this use of irony have on you as a reader?

The depiction of Caesar as a dangerous and powerful leader has relevance for all times and in all places.

TALES FROM THE STAGE
Theatrical Perspectives

The assassination of Caesar is one of the most dramatic moments in the play. The images on these pages show how various directors have chosen to present this scene.

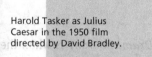

Harold Tasker as Julius Caesar in the 1950 film directed by David Bradley.

Brutus (Anthony Cochrane)
and Caesar (Robert Richmond)
in modern dress.
Aquila Theatre Company, 2000.

Dress rehearsal for 1912
production at Lyric Theatre.
Cleveland Press Shakespeare
Photographs.

The last and fatal blow comes from Brutus, and Caesar falls. The conspirators cry out "Liberty! Freedom! Tyranny is dead!" They immediately begin to explain their actions to the shocked senators and citizens nearby.

✱ CAESAR. *Et tu, Brutè?*—Then fall, Caesar.

[*He dies.*]

CINNA. Liberty! Freedom! Tyranny is dead!
    Run hence, proclaim, cry it about the streets.

CASSIUS. Some to the common pulpits and cry out   80
    "Liberty, freedom, and enfranchisement!"

BRUTUS. People and senators, be not affrighted.
    Fly not; stand still. Ambition's debt is paid.

77 *Et tu, Brutè:* You too, Brutus?

PERSONA ACTION

The personas onstage are stunned by Caesar's murder. Some scream, some cry; all leave the playing area quickly.

❓ Create director notes on how you would plot the pace and emotional pitch of this scene from the time Metellus kneels on page 95 until Caesar falls.

80 common pulpits: public speaking platforms

81 enfranchisement: the end of slavery

83 Ambition's debt: What Caesar owed to Rome for his ambition

Et tu, Brutè? Louis Calhern and James Mason, Mankiewicz film, 1953.

✱ "*Et tu, Brutè?*" says the dying Caesar to his assassin Brutus—meaning, "And thou, Brutus?" But according to the Roman biographer Suetonius, Caesar actually said (in Greek), "And thou, my son?" Suetonius believed a rumor that Brutus was actually Caesar's illegitimate (out-of-wedlock) son. Shakespeare's other historical source, Plutarch's *Lives*, also hinted that Brutus was really Caesar's son. So Caesar's actual final words may have expressed his horror at being slain by his own offspring.

As word spreads of Caesar's murder, chaos erupts. The conspirators decide to face the Roman citizens to explain their actions.

CASCA. Go to the pulpit, Brutus.

DECIUS.   And Cassius too.

BRUTUS. Where's Publius?   85

CINNA. Here, quite confounded with this mutiny.

METELLUS. Stand fast together, lest some friend of Caesar's
    Should chance—

BRUTUS. Talk not of standing.—Publius, good cheer.
    There is no harm intended to your person,   90
    Nor to no Roman else. So tell them, Publius.

CASSIUS. And leave us, Publius, lest that the people,
    Rushing on us, should do your age some mischief.

BRUTUS. Do so, and let no man abide this deed
    But we the doers.   95

[All but the conspirators exeunt. Enter TREBONIUS.]

✱ **CASSIUS.** Where is Antony?

TREBONIUS.   Fled to his house amaz'd.
    Men, wives, and children stare, cry out, and run
    As it were doomsday.

BRUTUS.   Fates, we will know your pleasures.
    That we shall die we know; 'tis but the time,
    And drawing days out, that men stand upon.   100

CASCA. Why, he that cuts off twenty years of life
    Cuts off so many years of fearing death.

---

86 confounded: confused;
mutiny: rebellion

89 standing: resistance

? What might old Publius be thinking here?

93 age: old age; **mischief:** injury

PERSONA ACTION

All personas scatter and race to the safety of their forums. They show horror or celebration depending on their loyalty.

94 abide: be responsible for

96 amaz'd: in shock

PERSONA JOURNAL

Describe what is happening in Rome as word of Caesar's death spreads.

100 drawing days ... upon: and the prolonging of life that men care about

---

✱ **Tongue-Tied?** So far, Antony's part has been one of the smallest in the play. During the first two and a half acts, Antony has only spoken 19 words! But throughout the rest of the play, his part will be very large. Overall, he has more lines than Caesar. Why do you think Shakespeare has kept Mark Antony in the background until this moment of the play?

Brutus asks that each conspirator wash his hands and smear his sword with Caesar's blood before they go to the Forum. As they do so, Cassius and Brutus consider how long history will remember them as the men who saved their country from a despot's rule.

BRUTUS. Grant that, and then is death a benefit.
  So are we Caesar's friends, that have abridg'd
✱ His time of fearing death. Stoop, Romans, stoop,   105
  And let us bathe our hands in Caesar's blood
  Up to the elbows and besmear our swords.
  Then walk we forth, even to the marketplace,
  And, waving our red weapons o'er our heads,
  Let's all cry "Peace, freedom, and liberty!"   110

CASSIUS. Stoop then, and wash. How many ages hence
  Shall this our lofty scene be acted over,
  In states unborn and accents yet unknown!

BRUTUS. How many times shall Caesar bleed in sport,
  That now on Pompey's basis lies along   115
  No worthier than the dust!

104 abridg'd: shortened

? Why do you think Brutus asks the conspirators to bathe their hands in Caesar's blood?

? Why are Cassius' lines, 111–113, ironic?

114 in sport: in a play

115 on Pompey's basis: at the base of Pompey's statue

The conspirators wash their hands in Caesar's blood. Royal Shakespeare Company, 1973.

✱ **Bloodbath** Since the 18th century, some editors have doubted that the idealistic Brutus would actually say the gory lines "Stoop, Romans, stoop,/And let us bathe our hands in Caesar's blood/Up to the elbows and besmear our swords." They think these lines and the rest of this speech were given to Brutus by a printer's error. They insist that these words should instead be spoken by the more cynical Casca. Do you agree or disagree that these lines are inappropriate for Brutus?

As the conspirators prepare to go to the marketplace, one of Antony's servants arrives bringing a message to Brutus. Antony requests safe passage to come and hear for himself why the conspirators felt it necessary to kill Caesar. Brutus gives his guarantee.

CASSIUS.   So oft as that shall be,
   So often shall the knot of us be call'd
   The men that gave their country liberty.

DECIUS. What, shall we forth?

CASSIUS.   Ay, every man away.
   Brutus shall lead, and we will grace his heels   120
   With the most boldest and best hearts of Rome.

[Enter a SERVANT.*]*

BRUTUS. Soft, who comes here? A friend of Antony's.

SERVANT.

[Kneeling.]

   Thus, Brutus, did my master bid me kneel.
   Thus did Mark Antony bid me fall down,
   And, being prostrate, thus he bade me say: 125
   Brutus is noble, wise, valiant, and honest;
   Caesar was mighty, bold, royal, and loving.
   Say, I love Brutus, and I honour him;
   Say, I fear'd Caesar, honoured him, and lov'd him.
   If Brutus will vouchsafe that Antony   130
   May safely come to him and be resolv'd
   How Caesar hath deserv'd to lie in death,
   Mark Antony shall not love Caesar dead
   So well as Brutus living, but will follow
   The fortunes and affairs of noble Brutus   135
   Through the hazards of this untrod state
   With all true faith. So says my master Antony.

BRUTUS. Thy master is a wise and valiant Roman.
   I never thought him worse.
   Tell him, so please him come unto this place,   140
   He shall be satisfied, and by my honour,
   Depart untouch'd.

117 knot: group

119 forth: leave

120 grace his heels: follow him

122 Soft: Wait a minute

❓ What do you think the servant is thinking and feeling here? Try saying the line with the emotion you described.

130 vouchsafe: guarantee
131 resolv'd: informed

136 untrod state: uncertain state of affairs

140 so please him come: if it pleases him to come

Cassius once again expresses his belief that Antony is dangerous. Antony arrives and is welcomed by Brutus. Antony at first registers shock at seeing Caesar's body and then speaks to the conspirators. He says that if they intend to kill him as well, they should do it now. He is ready to die alongside Caesar.

SERVANT.   I'll fetch him presently.

[Exit SERVANT.*]*

BRUTUS. I know that we shall have him well to friend.

CASSIUS. I wish we may; but yet have I a mind
✱ That fears him much, and my misgiving still   145
  Falls shrewdly to the purpose.

[Enter ANTONY.*]*

BRUTUS. But here comes Antony.—Welcome, Mark Antony!

ANTONY. O mighty Caesar, dost thou lie so low?
  Are all thy conquests, glories, triumphs, spoils,
  Shrunk to this little measure? Fare thee well.—   150
  I know not, gentlemen, what you intend,
  Who else must be let blood, who else is rank.
  If I myself, there is no hour so fit
  As Caesar's death's hour, nor no instrument
  Of half that worth as those your swords made rich 155
  With the most noble blood of all this world.
  I do beseech ye, if you bear me hard,
  Now, whilst your purpled hands do reek and smoke,
  Fulfill your pleasure. Live a thousand years,
  I shall not find myself so apt to die;   160
  No place will please me so, no mean of death,
  As here by Caesar, and by you cut off,
  The choice and master spirits of this age.

BRUTUS. O Antony, beg not your death of us!
  Though now we must appear bloody and cruel,   165
  As by our hands and this our present act

143 well to: as our

145–146 still/Falls … purpose: always turns out to be close to the truth

152 let blood: killed; **rank:** corrupt

155 made rich: enriched

157 bear me hard: have a grudge against me

158 do reek and smoke: are stained with Caesar's blood

159 Live: If I live

160 apt: ready

161 mean: means

163 choice and master: leading and strongest

❓ Do you think Antony is really ready to die?

✱ **Will the Wordsmith** Not only did Shakespeare add many quotable phrases and sayings to the language, he actually made up *words* that we still use today. For example, Cassius' use of "misgiving" (meaning a feeling of doubt or worry) is the earliest known use of that word in the English language.

Brutus and Cassius assure Antony that they have no intention of killing him and that he will even have a say in the formation of a new government. Brutus asks Antony to be patient while the conspirators calm the fears of the citizenry. Antony thanks the group and shakes the bloody hand of each one.

You see we do, yet see you but our hands
And this the bleeding business they have done.
Our hearts you see not; they are pitiful;
And pity to the general wrong of Rome   170
(As fire drives out fire, so pity pity)
Hath done this deed on Caesar. For your part,
To you our swords have leaden points, Mark Antony.
Our arms in strength of malice, and our hearts
Of brothers' temper, do receive you in   175
With all kind love, good thoughts, and reverence.

CASSIUS. Your voice shall be as strong as any man's
In the disposing of new dignities.

BRUTUS. Only be patient till we have appeas'd
The multitude, beside themselves with fear;   180
And then we will deliver you the cause
Why I, that did love Caesar when I struck him,
Have thus proceeded.

ANTONY.   I doubt not of your wisdom.
Let each man render me his bloody hand.
First, Marcus Brutus, will I shake with you.—   185
Next, Caius Cassius, do I take your hand.—
Now, Decius Brutus, yours;—now yours, Metellus;—
✱ Yours, Cinna;—and, my valiant Casca, yours;—
Though last, not least in love, yours, good Trebonius.
Gentlemen all—alas, what shall I say?   190
My credit now stands on such slippery ground
That one of two bad ways you must conceit me,
Either a coward or a flatterer.—
That I did love thee, Caesar, O, 'tis true!

168 bleeding: bloody
169 pitiful: full of pity

171 so pity pity: pity drives out pity

173 leaden: blunt

174–175 Our arms ... in: With our arms, which must seem to you steeped in evil, and with our hearts, full of brotherly affection, we receive you as one of us

176 reverence: respect

178 disposing of new dignities: forming of a new government

181 deliver: explain to

❓ What do you think about Antony and his willingness to shake hands with Caesar's murderers?

191 credit: credibility

192 conceit: regard

199 corse: corpse

✱ **A Cutting Remark** Casca might detect a note of sarcasm in Antony's reference to him as "my valiant Casca." While it's true that Casca was the first conspirator to stab Caesar, it's also true that he stabbed him in the back—hardly a "valiant" act.

Antony grieves for Caesar and asks forgiveness for making peace with his murderers. At this, Cassius asks if Antony should be considered a friend or an enemy. Antony replies that he is a friend, but he would like to know why the group thought Caesar was so dangerous.

If then thy spirit look upon us now,   195
Shall it not grieve thee dearer than thy death
To see thy Antony making his peace,
Shaking the bloody fingers of thy foes—
Most noble!—in the presence of thy corse?
Had I as many eyes as thou hast wounds,   200
Weeping as fast as they stream forth thy blood,
It would become me better than to close
In terms of friendship with thine enemies.
Pardon me, Julius! Here wast thou bay'd, brave hart,
Here didst thou fall, and here thy hunters stand   205
Sign'd in thy spoil and crimsoned in thy Lethe.
O world, thou wast the forest to this hart,
And this indeed, O world, the heart of thee.
How like a deer strucken by many princes
Dost thou here lie!   210

CASSIUS. Mark Antony—

ANTONY.   Pardon me, Caius Cassius.
The enemies of Caesar shall say this;
Then, in a friend, it is cold modesty.

CASSIUS. I blame you not for praising Caesar so.
But what compact mean you to have with us?   215
Will you be prick'd in number of our friends,
Or shall we on and not depend on you?

ANTONY. Therefore I took your hands, but was indeed
Sway'd from the point by looking down on Caesar.
Friends am I with you all and love you all,   220
Upon this hope, that you shall give me reasons
Why and wherein Caesar was dangerous.

202–203 become me … close/In: suit me better than to make

204 wast thou … hart: Where you were cornered, brave one (**hart:** stag)

206 Sign'd in … Lethe: Marked by your slaughter and bloody by your blood (In mythology, Lethe was a river in Hades.)

209 strucken: struck

❓ Is Antony risking anything by speaking in this manner? Why do you think he does so, and what is at stake?

213 in: for

215 compact mean you: agreement do you plan

216 prick'd in number: counted on as one

217 on: proceed

218 Therefore: That's why

❓ Antony says he is a friend to the conspirators. Do you believe him?

Brutus tells Antony that he will hear the reasons for Caesar's death, and that they will satisfy him. Antony asks to take Caesar's body to the marketplace and to speak at his funeral. Brutus agrees, despite Cassius' objections, but only on the condition that Brutus speaks first.

BRUTUS. Or else were this a savage spectacle.
    Our reasons are so full of good regard
    That were you, Antony, the son of Caesar,   225
    You should be satisfied.

ANTONY.   That's all I seek;
    And am, moreover, suitor that I may
    Produce his body to the market place,
    And in the pulpit, as becomes a friend,
    Speak in the order of his funeral.   230

BRUTUS. You shall, Mark Antony.

CASSIUS.   Brutus, a word with you.

✱ *[Aside to* BRUTUS.*]* You know not what you do. Do not consent
    That Antony speak in his funeral.
    Know you how much the people may be mov'd
    By that which he will utter?

BRUTUS. *[Aside to* CASSIUS.*]*   By your pardon—   235
    I will myself into the pulpit first
    And show the reason of our Caesar's death.
    What Antony shall speak I will protest
    He speaks by leave and by permission;
    And that we are contented Caesar shall   240
    Have all true rites and lawful ceremonies,
    It shall advantage more than do us wrong.

CASSIUS. *[Aside to* BRUTUS.*]* I know not what may fall. I like it not.

BRUTUS. Mark Antony, here, take you Caesar's body.
    You shall not in your funeral speech blame us,   245
    But speak all good you can devise of Caesar
    And say you do't by our permission,

223 Or else: Otherwise

224 so full of good regard: so good and so persuasive

227 And am, moreover, suitor: And I also request

228 Produce: Take

230 in the order of: during

❓ Why do you think Brutus quickly agrees to let Antony speak at Caesar's funeral ceremony?

236 myself into: speak myself in

238 protest: proclaim

242 advantage: be to our advantage

243 fall: happen

PERSONA JOURNAL

What do you know or have you heard about Antony? What kind of person is he?

✱ **Foreshadowing to the Max** Remember that *foreshadowing* refers to hints in the text about what will occur later in the plot. Cassius supplies lots of foreshadowing in this scene, especially when he warns Brutus not to let Antony speak at Caesar's funeral. Even readers and playgoers who don't know the story of *Julius Caesar* are likely to sense that Antony's funeral oration will lead to trouble for the conspirators.

Alone, Antony (Marlon Brando) vows revenge
for the death of Caesar. Mankiewicz film, 1953.

All the conspirators leave as Antony again addresses Caesar's corpse. He grieves and promises Caesar that his death will be avenged.

Else shall you not have any hand at all
About his funeral. And you shall speak
In the same pulpit whereto I am going,   250
After my speech is ended.

ANTONY.   Be it so.
I do desire no more.

BRUTUS. Prepare the body then, and follow us.

[Exeunt. ANTONY *remains.]*

ANTONY. O pardon me, thou bleeding piece of earth,
That I am meek and gentle with these butchers.   255
Thou art the ruins of the noblest man
That ever livèd in the tide of times.
Woe to the hand that shed this costly blood!
Over thy wounds now do I prophesy
(Which like dumb mouths do ope their ruby lips   260
To beg the voice and utterance of my tongue)
A curse shall light upon the limbs of men;
Domestic fury and fierce civil strife
Shall cumber all the parts of Italy;
Blood and destruction shall be so in use   265
And dreadful objects so familiar
That mothers shall but smile when they behold
Their infants quarter'd with the hands of war,
All pity chok'd with custom of fell deeds;
And Caesar's spirit, ranging for revenge,   270
With Atè by his side com hot from hell,
Shall in these confines with a monarch's voice
✱ Cry "Havoc!" and let slip the dogs of war,
That this foul deed shall smell above the earth
With carrion men, groaning for burial.   275

257 tide of times: course of history

260 dumb: silent; **ope:** open

PERSONA JOURNAL

Tell about a curse that you have heard about and what happened because of it.

264 cumber: overwhelm

265 in use: common

268 quarter'd: cut to pieces

269 custom of fell deeds: the frequency of these cruel acts

270 ranging: hunting

271 Atè: The goddess of discord and vengeance in Greek Mythology

272 confines: places

273 let slip: unleash

275 carrion men: decaying bodies

❓ For this speech Antony is alone on stage with Caesar's body. Describe two different ways he could play these lines.

✱ **"The Dogs of War"** In the prologue of Shakespeare's history play *Henry V*, probably written earlier the same year as *Julius Caesar* (1599), the playwright names the dogs of war. They are famine, sword, and fire. "Havoc!" was the cry generals used to signal the slaughter and pillaging of the enemy.

One of Octavius' servants enters to tell Antony that Octavius, Caesar's nephew and heir, is on his way to Rome as Caesar had requested. The servant is shocked to see Caesar's body. Antony tells the servant to accompany him to the marketplace, witness the funeral, and then quickly ride back to Octavius and tell him all that has happened.

[Enter Octavio's SERVANT.*]*

You serve Octavius Caesar, do you not?

SERVANT. I do, Mark Antony.

ANTONY. Caesar did write for him to come to Rome.

SERVANT. He did receive his letters and is coming,
       And bid me to say to you by word of mouth—   280
       O Caesar!

ANTONY. Thy heart is big. Get thee apart and weep.
       Passion, I see is catching, for mine eyes,
       Seeing those beds of sorrow stand in thine,
       Began to water. Is thy master coming?   285

SERVANT. He lies tonight within seven leagues of Rome.

ANTONY. Post back with speed, and tell him what hath chanc'd.
       Here is a mourning Rome, a dangerous Rome,
       No Rome of safety for Octavius yet;
       Hie hence and tell him so.—Yet stay awhile;   290
       Thou shalt not back till I have borne this corpse
       Into the marketplace. There I shall try,
       In my oration, how the people take
       The cruel issue of these bloody men,
       According to the which thou shalt discourse   295
       To young Octavius of the state of things.
       Lend me your hand.

[Exeunt with CAESAR'S *body.]*

> **?** How might Antony react if he did not recognize Octavius' servant immediately?

282 big: full of grief

283 Passion: Sorrow

284 beds: tears

286 seven leagues: about 21 miles

287 Post: Ride away; **hath chanc'd:** has happened

290 Hie: Go

292 try: test

294 issue: results

295–296 which thou … To: success of my speech, you shall inform

LOYALTY CHECK

Will you stay where you are or switch sides?

Setting the Scene
JULIUS CAESAR
Act III, Scenes ii and iii *or* Crowd Control

Critical Query: How do Brutus and Antony manipulate the crowds?

Word Play: Rhetoric

Rhetoric is the art of communicating effectively, either in writing or in speech. It uses persuasive techniques such as repetition, strong imagery, rhythm, diction (word choice), and emotional appeals. Scene ii contains some of the most powerful speeches ever written. Watch for the rhetorical techniques used by the speakers.

Warm-Up Improv

Two of your friends are having an argument over who was at fault in a recent car accident. As first one, then the other, tells you his or her version, you are swayed to believe them.

Famous Quotes from Scene ii

- . . .not that I loved Caesar less, but that I loved Rome more.
- Friends, Romans, and countrymen, lend me your ears.
- The evil that men do lives after them. . .
- Brutus is an honourable man. . .
- This was the most unkindest cut of all. . .

Behind the Scene: Caesar's Funeral

Common practice would have had Caesar cremated in the Martian Fields outside the city, but the volatile crowd, after hearing the contents of his will, decided to do him greater honor by cremating his body in the center of the Forum. Torches from the funeral pyre were used to burn down the houses of the conspirators. Several years later a temple was built at the Forum to honor Caesar with an altar on the spot where his body was burned. The remains of the altar can still be seen and, curiously, fresh flowers can be found there almost every day.

From the Prop Box

- Cloak for Caesar's body
- Caesar's will
- Flashlights to be used as torches

Classroom Set Design

A two-forum setup is used with the teacher's desk serving as the speaker's platform. Two or three chairs in front of the platform can be used as the bier where Antony places Caesar's body. (Use a cloak or robe to indicate the body.) Brutus and Cassius enter and exit from stage right. Antony enters from the center aisle. Caesarians and Pompeians stand in their forums as they listen and react to the speakers.

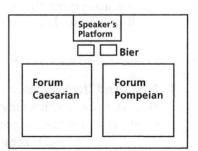

In the Roman Forum, Brutus and Cassius face a mob of Roman citizens. They decide to split the crowd into two groups to give an accounting of Caesar's death. Cassius leads one group away as Brutus begins by telling the other group that he too loved Caesar, but he loved Rome more.

Scene ii. Rome. The Forum

[Enter BRUTUS *and* CASSIUS, *with the* PLEBEIANS.*]*

ALL. We will be satisfied! Let us be satisfied!

BRUTUS. Then follow me and give me audience, friends.—
　　Cassius, go you into the other street,
　　And part the numbers.—
　　Those that will hear me speak, let 'em stay here;　　　5
　　Those that will follow Cassius, go with him;
　　And public reasons shall be renderèd
　　Of Caesar's death.

FIRST PLEBEIAN.　　　I will hear Brutus speak.

SECOND PLEBEIAN. I will hear Cassius, and compare their reasons
　　When severally we hear them renderèd.　　　10

[Exit Cassius, with some of the PLEBEIANS. *Brutus goes into the pulpit.]*

THIRD PLEBEIAN. The noble Brutus is ascended. Silence.

✱ **BRUTUS.** Be patient till the last.
　　Romans, countrymen, and lovers, hear me for my cause,
　　and be silent, that you may hear. Believe me for mine
　　honour, and have respect to mine honour, that you may　　　15
　　believe. Censure me in your wisdom, and awake your
　　senses, that you may the better judge. If there be any in
　　this assembly, any dear friends of Caesar's, to him I say
　　that Brutus' love to Caesar was no less than his. If then
　　that friend demand why Brutus rose against Caesar, this is　　　20
　　my answer: not that I loved Caesar less, but that I loved
　　Rome more. Had you rather Caesar were living, and die

PERSONA ACTION

The third and fourth group of personas enters.

PERSONA ACTION

All personas mutter responses and contribute to crowd noise whenever the character designation ALL appears in this scene.

1 will be satisfied: insist on a full explanation

2 give me audience: listen to me

PERSONA JOURNAL

What is your reaction to seeing the conspirators with their weapons and hands covered in Caesar's blood?

4 part the numbers: divide the crowd

7 public reasons: an official account

10 severally: separately

PERSONA ACTION

Several personas from each group onstage leave with Cassius. All others stand in place to hear Brutus.

11 is ascended: has climbed to the platform

13 lovers: dear friends

16 Censure: Judge

✱ **Prose and Verse** Although most of *Julius Caesar* is written in verse, Shakespeare also sometimes uses *prose* (language without rhythmic structure). When justifying Caesar's assassination to the crowd, Brutus speaks almost entirely in prose. Later, when Mark Antony stirs the crowd to revenge, he speaks in verse. As you read this scene, consider why Shakespeare had Brutus speak in prose and Antony speak in verse.

Brutus continues to explain that it was Caesar's ambition that caused him and others to take action for the good of Rome.

all slaves, than that Caesar were dead, to live all freemen?
As Caesar loved me, I weep for him. As he was fortunate,
I rejoice at it. As he was valiant, I honour him. But, as he   25
was ambitious, I slew him. There is tears for his love, joy
for his fortune, honour for his valor, and death for his
ambition. Who is here so base that would be a bondman?
If any, speak, for him have I offended. Who is here so rude
that would not be a Roman? If any, speak, for him have I   30
offended. Who is here so vile that will not love his country?
If any, speak, for him have I offended. I pause for a reply.

23 all: as; **all freemen:** as free men

28 base: vile; **bondman:** slave
29 rude: uncivilized

PERSONA ACTION

Groups respond to Brutus' speech at various times.

James Mason as Brutus. Mankiewicz film, 1953.

The crowd cheers for Brutus as Antony enters with Caesar's body.

Act III Scene ii

ALL. None, Brutus, none.

BRUTUS. Then none have I offended. I have done no more to
Caesar than you shall do to Brutus. The question of his   35
death is enrolled in the Capitol, his glory not extenuated,
where in he was worthy, nor his offenses enforced for
which he suffered death.

[Enter MARK ANTONY, *with* CAESAR'S BODY.]

Here comes his body, mourned by Mark Antony, who,
though he had no hand in his death, shall receive the   40
benefit of his dying—a place in the commonwealth—as
which of you shall not? With this I depart: that, as I slew
my best lover for the good of Rome, I have the same
dagger for myself when it shall please my country to
need my death.   45

ALL. Live, Brutus, live, live!

FIRST PLEBEIAN. Bring him with triumph home unto his house.

SECOND PLEBEIAN. Give him a statue with his ancestors.

✱ **THIRD PLEBEIAN.** Let him be Caesar.

FOURTH PLEBEIAN.   Caesar's better parts   50
Shall be crown'd in Brutus.

FIRST PLEBEIAN.   We'll bring him to his house
with shouts and clamours.

BRUTUS.   My countrymen—

SECOND PLEBEIAN. Peace, silence! Brutus speaks.

FIRST PLEBEIAN.   Peace, ho!

PERSONA JOURNAL

How do you feel about Brutus and
the conspirators now?

35–36 The question ... enrolled:
The reasons for his death are
written down; **extenuated:**
diminished

38 enforced: overstated

41 place: position

43 best lover: closest friend

❓ How do you think Brutus feels
about the crowd calling for him to
be the new Caesar?

✱ **King Brutus?** Brutus has just led a brutal conspiracy to assassinate a would-be king and save the
republic of Rome. But now, the plebeians are talking about making Brutus himself a king. "Let him be
Caesar," one says. "Caesar's better parts/Shall be crown'd in Brutus," says another. Does Brutus hear
these remarks? If so, how do you think he feels about them?

Brutus urges the crowd to pay their respects to Caesar's body and to hear Antony speak.

BRUTUS. Good countrymen, let me depart alone,
And, for my sake, stay here with Antony.   55
Do grace to Caesar's corpse, and grace his speech
Tending to Caesar's glories, which Mark Antony
(By our permission) is allow'd to make.
I do entreat you, not a man depart
Save I alone, till Antony have spoke.   60

[He descends and exits.]

FIRST PLEBEIAN. Stay, ho, and let us hear Mark Antony!

THIRD PLEBEIAN. Let him go up into the public chair.

ALL. We'll hear him.—Noble Antony, go up.

ANTONY. For Brutus' sake, I am beholding to you.

✳ *[He goes into the pulpit.]*

FOURTH PLEBEIAN. What does he say of Brutus?

THIRD PLEBEIAN.   He says, for Brutus' sake   65
He finds himself beholding to us all.

FOURTH PLEBEIAN. 'Twere best he speak no harm of Brutus here.

FIRST PLEBEIAN. This Caesar was a tyrant.

THIRD PLEBEIAN.   Nay, that's certain.
We are blest that Rome is rid of him.

SECOND PLEBEIAN. Peace! Let us hear what Antony can say.   70

ANTONY. You gentle Romans—

ALL.   Peace, ho! Let us hear him.

---

56 Do grace to: Honor; **grace his speech:** and honor Antony's speech

LOYALTY CHECK

Has Brutus' speech changed your mind about the death of Caesar?

62 chair: platform

PERSONA JOURNAL

Describe Antony as he climbs to the platform to speak.

64 beholding to: indebted

PERSONA ACTION

Groups react to Antony as he prepares to speak.

✳ **Oration Location** The stage directions say that both Brutus and Antony go "into the pulpit" to speak. But Shakespeare didn't write these directions; they were added by an editor. However, Brutus and Antony are described in the dialogue as "ascending" to make their speeches. So did they speak from the gallery above the stage? Possibly, but the gallery was often used for audience seating instead of dramatic scenes. Brutus and Antony may have gone to a pulpit or "public chair" upstage—that is, farther back on the stage.

Antony begins to eulogize Caesar. He says if Caesar was in fact ambitious, then he has paid for it most dearly. He goes on to list many examples of Caesar's behavior that show him as anything but ambitious.

✱ ANTONY. Friends, Romans, countrymen, lend me your ears.
    I come to bury Caesar, not to praise him.
    The evil that men do lives after them;
    The good is oft interrèd with their bones.   75
    So let it be with Caesar. The noble Brutus
    Hath told you Caesar was ambitious.
    If it were so, it was a grievous fault,
    And grievously hath Caesar answer'd it.
    Here, under leave of Brutus and the rest   80
    (For Brutus is an honourable man;
    So are they all, all honourable men)
    Come I to speak in Caesar's funeral.
    He was my friend, faithful and just to me,
    But Brutus says he was ambitious,   85
    And Brutus is an honourable man.
    He hath brought many captives home to Rome,
    Whose ransoms did the general coffers fill.
    Did this in Caesar seem ambitious?
    When that the poor have cried, Caesar hath wept;   90
    Ambition should be made of sterner stuff.
    Yet Brutus says he was ambitious,
    And Brutus is an honourable man.

❓ What does Antony hope to accomplish with his speech?

75 oft interrèd: often buried

78 grievous: terrible

79 grievously: terribly; **answer'd:** paid for

80 under leave: with the permission

84 He: Caesar

88 general coffers: national treasury

TALES FROM THE STAGE

In 1963, actress Penelope Keith got a modest start as a bit player in a production of *Julius Caesar*. The director had instructed crowd members to react realistically, saying whatever they felt appropriate. So when Antony exclaimed, "lend me your ears," Ms. Keith pertly replied, "Have an ear." She thought her remark would be muffled in the crowd noise and was embarrassed when the famous critic Kenneth Tynan blisteringly condemned her improvised line in his review the next day.

But Keith's fellow actors gave her a round of applause when she showed up for the next performance. It was the first time Tynan had ever mentioned a bit player in any of his reviews!

You all did see that on the Lupercal
I thrice presented him a kingly crown,   95
Which he did thrice refuse. Was this ambition?
Yet Brutus says he was ambitious,
And sure he is an honourable man.
I speak not to disprove what Brutus spoke,
But here I am to speak what I do know.   100
You all did love him once, not without cause.
What cause withholds you then to mourn for him?—
O judgment, thou art fled to brutish beasts,
And men have lost their reason!—Bear with me;
My heart is in the coffin there with Caesar,   105
And I must pause till it come back to me.

[He weeps.]

94 Lupercal: the recent feast day
(See bottom of page 28.)

102 withholds you then: keeps
you from

Antony (Marlon Brando)
speaks to the citizens of
Rome. Mankiewicz, 1953.

? Is he really weeping?

Brando Bashing   In the 1950s, Marlon Brando was known as the ultimate American "method" actor—one who could express emotions with blazing intensity. Most of his roles were working-class ruffians and rebels. But could he do Shakespeare? In 1953, he played Antony in a film version of *Julius Caesar*. Most critics praised his performance, and he received an Oscar nomination for it. But there have been dissenters. Shakespearean scholar Bernard Grebanier said that Brando spoke as if his "mouth were filled with mashed potatoes."

Several people in the crowd begin to question the actions of the conspirators. Others express their belief that Antony is truthful and Caesar has been wrongly assassinated. Antony speaks again and holds up Caesar's will.

FIRST PLEBEIAN. Methinks there is much reason in his sayings.

SECOND PLEBEIAN. If thou consider rightly of the matter,
Caesar has had great wrong.

THIRD PLEBEIAN.   Has he, masters?
I fear there will a worse come in his place.   110

FOURTH PLEBEIAN. Mark'd ye his words? He would not take
the crown;
Therefore 'tis certain he was not ambitious.

FIRST PLEBEIAN. If it be found so, some will dear abide it.

SECOND PLEBEIAN. Poor soul, his eyes are red as fire with weeping.

✱ **THIRD PLEBEIAN.** There's not a nobler man in Rome than Antony. 115

FOURTH PLEBEIAN. Now mark him. He begins again to speak.

ANTONY. But yesterday the word of Caesar might
Have stood against the world. Now lies he there,
And none so poor to do him reverence.
O masters, if I were dispos'd to stir   120
Your hearts and minds to mutiny and rage,
I should do Brutus wrong and Cassius wrong,
Who (you all know) are honourable men.
I will not do them wrong. I rather choose
To wrong the dead, to wrong myself and you,   125
Than I will wrong such honourable men.
But here's a parchment with the seal of Caesar.
I found it in his closet. 'Tis his will.

109 Caesar has … wrong: wrong was done to Caesar; **masters:** comrades

110 worse: worse ruler

113 dear abide it: pay dearly for it

116 mark: listen to

119 none so … reverence: no one is humble enough to pay him his due respect

120 dispos'd: inclined

127 parchment: document

128 closet: study

PERSONA JOURNAL

How is Antony's speech affecting you?

✱ **No Small Parts** Even Shakespeare's nameless characters are vividly drawn, with individual quirks and characteristics. The Third Plebeian, for example, is portrayed as easily persuaded by any orator that comes along. A while back, he said of Brutus, "Let him be Caesar." But now he's singing a different tune: "There's not a nobler man in Rome than Antony."

Antony tells the crowd that if they were to hear Caesar's will, they would make every effort to show honor and respect to Caesar. The crowd begs him to read the will. Antony refuses, saying that if the crowd knew that they were Caesar's heirs, he could not be responsible for what they might do.

Let but the commons hear this testament,
Which, pardon me, I do not mean to read,   130
And they would go and kiss dead Caesar's wounds,
And dip their napkins in his sacred blood—
Yea, beg a hair of him for memory,
And, dying, mention it within their wills,
Bequeathing it as a rich legacy   135
Unto their issue.

FOURTH PLEBEIAN. We'll hear the will. Read it, Mark Antony.

ALL. The will, the will! We will hear Caesar's will.

ANTONY. Have patience, gentle friends. I must not read it.
It is not meet you know how Caesar lov'd you.   140
You are not wood, you are not stones, but men.
And, being men, hearing the will of Caesar,
It will inflame you; it will make you mad.
'Tis good you know not that you are his heirs,
For if you should, O, what would come of it?   145

FOURTH PLEBEIAN. Read the will! We'll hear it, Antony.

ALL. You shall read us the will, Caesar's will.

ANTONY. Will you patient? Will you stay awhile?
I have o'ershot myself to tell you of it.
✱ I fear I wrong the honourable men   150
Whose daggers have stabb'd Caesar. I do fear it.

FOURTH PLEBEIAN. They were traitors. Honourable men?

ALL. The will! The testament!

SECOND PLEBEIAN. They were villains, murderers. The will!
Read the will.   155

---

129 commons: public; **testament:** will

132 napkins: handkerchiefs

135–136 Bequeathing ... issue: Passing it on as a precious gift to their children

140 meet: proper

PERSONA JOURNAL

What do you think is in Caesar's will?

149 o'ershot myself: gone too far

✱ **Verbal Irony** *Verbal irony* is when a person says one thing and means another. Antony's speeches to the crowd during Caesar's funeral are among the most famous examples of verbal irony in all drama. He begins by saying, "I come to bury Caesar, not to praise him"—then goes on to praise Caesar lavishly. He also repeatedly calls Brutus and the conspirators "honourable men," even while making them sound like vicious traitors. How does Antony's use of verbal irony add to his success at manipulating the crowd?

The crowd gathers around Caesar's body, and Antony joins them. He points out where each of the traitors stabbed Caesar.

Act III   Scene ii

ANTONY. You will compel me, then, to read the will?
　　Then make a ring about the corpse of Caesar,
　　And let me show you him that made the will.
　　Shall I descend? And will you give me leave?

ALL. Come down.　　　　　　　　　　　　　　　　160

SECOND PLEBEIAN. Descend.

THIRD PLEBEIAN. You shall have leave.

[ANTONY descends.]

FOURTH PLEBEIAN. A ring; stand round.

FIRST PLEBEIAN. Stand from the hearse. Stand from the body.

SECOND PLEBEIAN. Room for Antony, most noble Antony.　　165

ANTONY. Nay, press not so upon me. Stand far off.

ALL. Stand back! Room! Bear back!

ANTONY. If you have tears, prepare to shed them now.
✱　You all do know this mantle. I remember
　　The first time ever Caesar put it on.　　　　　　170
　　'Twas on a summer's evening in his tent,
　　That day he overcame the Nervii.
　　Look, in this place ran Cassius' dagger through.
　　See what a rent the envious Casca made.
　　Through this the well-belovèd Brutus stabb'd,　　175
　　And, as he pluck'd his cursèd steel away,
　　Mark how the blood of Caesar follow'd it,
　　As rushing out of doors to be resolv'd
　　If Brutus so unkindly knock'd or no;

164 hearse: bier or coffin

166 far off: further away

169 mantle: cloak

172 Nervii: In 57 B.C., Caesar was victorious over this fierce tribe in Gaul.

174 rent: rip; **envious:** malicious

178 to be resolv'd: to make certain

✱ **Fact or Fiction?** Antony plays fast and loose with facts throughout this speech. He wasn't with Caesar on that "summer's evening" of the battle against the Nervii, when Caesar supposedly wore the cloak for the first time. And how can he tell the crowd which conspirators made which wounds in the cloak, not having witnessed Caesar's murder himself? While Antony's grief for Caesar is certainly genuine, he is not the most truthful character in the play.

Nicholas Farrell as Antony shows Caesar's bloody cloak to the crowd.
Royal Shakespeare Company, 1987.

Antony emphasizes that Brutus' blow was the most painful for
Caesar, as he dearly loved Brutus. Antony continues to play to the
crowd's sympathy and the horror of this traitorous act as he pulls off
Caesar's cloak to reveal his bloody, mangled body. The crowd erupts,
calling for revenge.

> For Brutus, as you know, was Caesar's angel.   180
> Judge, O you gods, how dearly Caesar lov'd him!
> This was the most unkindest cut of all;
> For when the noble Caesar saw him stab,
> Ingratitude, more strong than traitor's arms,
> Quite vanquish'd him. Then burst his mighty heart,   185
> And, in his mantle muffling up his face,
> Even at the base of Pompey's statue
> (Which all the while ran blood) great Caesar fell.
> O, what a fall was there, my countrymen!
> Then I and you and all of us fell down,   190
> Whilst bloody treason flourish'd over us.
> O now you weep, and I perceive you feel
> The dint of pity. These are gracious drops.
> Kind souls, what, weep you when you but behold
> Our Caesar's vesture wounded? Look you here,   195

✱ [ANTONY *lifts Caesar's cloak.*]

> Here is himself, marr'd as you see with traitors.

FIRST PLEBEIAN. O piteous spectacle!

SECOND PLEBEIAN. O noble Caesar!

THIRD PLEBEIAN. O woeful day!

FOURTH PLEBEIAN. O traitors, villains!   200

FIRST PLEBEIAN. O most bloody sight!

SECOND PLEBEIAN. We will be revenged.

ALL. Revenge! About! Seek! Burn! Fire! Kill!
> Slay! Let not a traitor live!

ANTONY. Stay, countrymen.   205

180 angel: favorite friend

182 most unkindest: most
unnatural or cruelest

PERSONA JOURNAL

What is your reaction to the sight
of Caesar's body?

186 mantle: cloak

193 dint: force

195 vesture: garment

196 marr'd: mutilated

✱ **Source Citation** Here's an excerpt from Plutarch's *Lives*, briefly describing Antony's funeral speech.
"[Antony] made a funeral oration in commendation of Caesar, according to the ancient custom of
praising noble men at their funerals. When he saw that the people were very glad and desirous also to
hear Caesar spoken of, and his praises uttered, he mingled his oration with lamentable words, and by
amplifying of matters did greatly move their hearts and affections unto pity and compassion."

Antony again speaks to the crowd, humbling himself and utilizing his abilities to incite their emotions. With false modesty he claims that Brutus is a much more eloquent speaker—one who could truly move them to mutiny. The crowd becomes more enraged.

FIRST PLEBEIAN. Peace there! Hear the noble Antony.

SECOND PLEBEIAN. We'll hear him, we'll follow him, we'll die
  with him.

✳ **ANTONY.** Good friends, sweet friends, let me not stir you up
  To such a sudden flood of mutiny.   210
  They that have done this deed are honourable.
  What private griefs they have, alas, I know not,   **212 griefs:** grudges
  That made them do it. They are wise and honourable,
  And will no doubt with reasons answer you.
  I come not, friends, to steal away your hearts.   215
  I am no orator, as Brutus is,
  But, as you know me all, a plain blunt man
  That love my friend, and that they know full well
  That gave me public leave to speak of him.   **219 public leave:** permission
  For I have neither wit, nor words, nor worth,   220   **220 wit:** intelligence
  Action, nor utterance, nor the power of speech   **221 Action:** Knowledge of gesture;
  To stir men's blood. I only speak right on.   **utterance:** delivery of speech
  I tell you that which you yourselves do know,
  Show you sweet Caesar's wounds, poor poor dumb mouths,
  And bid them speak for me. But were I Brutus,   225
  And Brutus Antony, there were an Antony   **226 there were:** that would be
  Would ruffle up your spirits and put a tongue   **227 ruffle:** stir
  In every wound of Caesar that should move
  The stones of Rome to rise and mutiny.

ALL. We'll mutiny.   230

FIRST PLEBEIAN. We'll burn the house of Brutus.

THIRD PLEBEIAN. Away, then. Come, seek the conspirators.

✳ **Rhetorical Tools** Antony's use of *irony* reaches its height when he dares to say, "I am no orator, as Brutus is ..." Antony has just delivered a series of truly stunning orations that have turned the crowd against Brutus and the conspirators. Also, note Antony's mastery of rhetorical devices like *oxymorons*, or pairings of contradictory words, as when he describes Caesar's wounds as "dumb mouths."

Antony reminds the crowd that they have not yet heard Caesar's will. He says that Caesar has left money to every Roman citizen and has also directed that his lands and gardens be made into public parks for all of Rome to share. The furious crowd storms off to burn the houses of the traitors.

ANTONY. Yet hear me, countrymen; yet hear me speak.

PLEBEIANS. Peace, ho! Hear Antony, most noble Antony!

ANTONY. Why, friends, you go to do you know not what.   235
　　Wherein hath Caesar thus deserv'd your loves?
　　Alas, you know not. I must tell you then.
　　You have forgot the will I told you of.

PLEBEIANS. Most true. The will! Let's stay and hear the will.

✱ **ANTONY.** Here is the will, and under Caesar's seal: 240
　　To every Roman citizen he gives,
　　To every several man, seventy-five drachmas.

SECOND PLEBEIANS. Most noble Caesar! We'll revenge his death.

THIRD PLEBEIAN. O royal Caesar!

ANTONY. Hear me with patience.   245

PLEBEIANS. Peace, ho!

ANTONY. Moreover, he hath left you all his walks,
　　His private arbours, and new-planted orchards,
　　On this side Tiber. He hath left them you,
　　And to your heirs forever—common pleasures   250
　　To walk abroad and recreate yourselves.
　　Here was a Caesar! When comes such another?

FIRST PLEBEIAN. Never, never!—Come, away, away!
　　We'll burn his body in the holy place
　　And with the brands fire the traitors' houses.   255
　　Take up the body.

SECOND PLEBEIAN. Go fetch fire.

242 several: single; **drachmas:** ancient Greek coins—75 would be approximately $100.

247 walks: pathways

248 orchards: gardens

250 common pleasures: as public parks

254 holy place: temple

255 brands: torches

❓ List all the persuasive techniques used by Antony during this scene. (See page III.)

✱ **Will Power** Although it's smart not to believe everything Antony says, he's not making up the contents of Caesar's will. According to Plutarch, Caesar "bequeathed unto every citizen of Rome 75 drachmas a man, and that he left his gardens and arbors unto the people, which he had on this side of the river of Tiber ..."

Antony reads Caesar's will to the crowd.
Royal Shakespeare Company, 1983.

Antony is pleased with his ability to incite the crowd to action. Octavius' servant returns with news that Octavius is now in Rome and that Brutus and Cassius have fled the city.

THIRD PLEBEIAN. Pluck down benches.

FOURTH PLEBEIAN. Pluck down forms, windows, anything.

[Exit PLEBEIANS *with Caesar's body.]*

ANTONY. Now let it work. Mischief, thou art afoot;   260
Take thou what course thou wilt.

[Enter SERVANT.*]*

                                 How now, fellow?

SERVANT. Sir, Octavius is already come to Rome.

ANTONY. Where is he?

SERVANT. He and Lepidus are at Caesar's home.

ANTONY. And thither will I straight to visit him.   265
He comes upon a wish. Fortune is merry,
And in this mood will give us anything.

SERVANT. I heard him say Brutus and Cassius
Are rid like madmen through the gates of Rome.

ANTONY. Belike they had some notice of the people   270
How I had mov'd them. Bring me to Octavius.

[Exeunt.]

---

259 forms: benches; **windows:** shutters

LOYALTY CHECK

Has Antony's speech convinced you to be a Caesarian?

264 Lepidus: Marcus Aemilius Lepidus, a supporter of Caesar

265 thither will I straight: I will go immediately

266 upon a: according to my

269 Are rid: Have ridden

270 Belike: Probably

Cinna, a poet, meets some of the angry crowd just coming from the Forum. They question him and want to know if he is a friend of Caesar's or an enemy.

Scene iii. Rome. A street

✳ *[Enter* CINNA THE POET, *and after him the* PLEBEIANS.*]*

CINNA. I dreamt tonight that I did feast with Caesar,
  And things unluckily charge my fantasy.
  I have no will to wander forth of doors,
  Yet something leads me forth.

FIRST PLEBEIAN. What is your name?   5

SECOND PLEBEIAN. Whither are you going?

THIRD PLEBEIAN. Where do you dwell?

FOURTH PLEBEIAN. Are you a married man or a bachelor?

SECOND PLEBEIAN. Answer every man directly.

FIRST PLEBEIAN. Ay, and briefly.   10

FOURTH PLEBEIAN. Ay, and wisely.

THIRD PLEBEIAN. Ay, and truly, you were best.

CINNA. What is my name? Whither am I going? Where do I
  dwell? Am I a married man or a bachelor? Then to answer
  every man directly and briefly, wisely and truly: wisely I say,   15
  I am a bachelor.

SECOND PLEBEIAN. That's as much as to say they are fools
  that marry. You'll bear me a bang for that, I fear. Proceed
  directly.

CINNA. Directly, I am going to Caesar's funeral.   20

FIRST PLEBEIAN. As a friend or an enemy?

---

1 tonight: last night

2 unluckily charge my fantasy: burden my imagination with bad omens

3 forth of doors: about the street

PERSONA ACTION

A small group of personas enters and reacts with the Plebeians who have dialogue.

12 you were best: if you know what's good for you

18 bear me a bang: receive a punch from me

✳ **Mob Violence** This short scene, with its mixture of grotesque comedy and frightful violence, has shocked audiences and readers for centuries. What do you think Shakespeare is saying here about the nature of mob violence? Should the murder of Cinna the poet be blamed on the plebeians or on Antony for having driven them out of control?

The brutal death of Cinna the poet. The Royal Shakespeare Company, 1972.

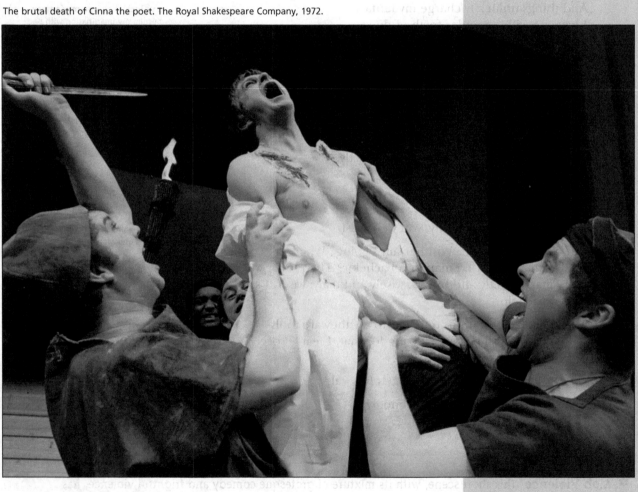

The crowd demands to know the poet's name. In a stroke of terrible irony, he has the same name as one of the conspirators. Cinna tries to tell the mob that he had nothing to do with Caesar's assassination, but his arguments fall on deaf ears, and the murderous crowd begins to tear him to pieces.

CINNA. As a friend.

SECOND PLEBEIAN. The matter is answered directly.

FOURTH PLEBEIAN. For your dwelling—briefly.

CINNA. Briefly, I dwell by the Capitol.   25

THIRD PLEBEIAN. Your name, sir, truly.

CINNA. Truly, my name is Cinna.

FIRST PLEBEIAN. Tear him to pieces! He's a conspirator.

CINNA. I am Cinna the poet, I am Cinna the poet!

FOURTH PLEBEIAN. Tear him for his bad verses, tear him for   30
his bad verses!

CINNA. I am not Cinna the conspirator.

FOURTH PLEBEIAN. It is no matter. His name's Cinna. Pluck
but his name out of his heart, and turn him going.

THIRD PLEBEIAN. Tear him, tear him! Come, brands, ho,   35
firebrands! To Brutus', to Cassius', burn all! Some to Decius'
house and some to Casca's, some to Ligarius'. Away, go!

[Exeunt all the PLEBEIANS *carrying off* CINNA.*]*

24 For your dwelling: Where is your home

? Imagine Cinna's reaction here. How would you portray this character?

34 turn him going: send him away

35 brands: torches

PERSONA ACTION

Onstage plebeians "attack" Cinna and carry him offstage.

PERSONA JOURNAL

In the years to come, how will you describe this day to your grandchildren?

Reacting to Act III

Analysis

1. What is the dramatic effect of the opening dialogue in Scene i?

2. What change do we see in Antony during his soliloquy over Caesar's corpse?

3. Why does Brutus' speech in Scene ii ultimately fail?

4. Antony's speech turns the crowd against the conspirators. But what might have happened if Brutus and Cassius had refused to let Antony speak to the crowd? Think about some possible outcomes and be ready to discuss them with the class.

5. Cinna the poet is murdered on the street by the mob even though he is not Lucius Cornelius Cinna, the conspirator. Do you think a single citizen would have attacked Cinna as opposed to a mob? Explain why or why not.

6. After Caesar's murder, what kind of leader does Rome most desperately need? Decide which of the two funeral orators—Brutus or Antony—is the better leader and explain your opinion.

Literary Elements

1. In Scene i, Antony predicts that Caesar's death will cause terrible things to happen. Look at lines 259–275 and note what effects he foresees as a result of Caesar's assassination.

2. **Rhetoric** is effective communication in writing or in speech. Compare the speeches of Brutus and Antony at Caesar's funeral and decide what makes one of them more effective than the other. Look for persuasive techniques such as **repetition**, strong **imagery**, **rhythm**, **diction** (word choice), and **emotional appeals**, in addition to others. Which speaker do the Roman crowds find more believable?

3. In Scene i, Brutus says, "Stoop, Romans, stoop. And let us bathe our hands in Caesar's blood up to the elbows and besmear our swords." After this they march to the marketplace and cry for "Peace, freedom, and liberty!" Does this **imagery** strike you as an effective way to summon sympathy for their cause? Explain why or why not.

Writing

1. In Scene ii, Cassius goes off to give his own speech about the reasons for killing Caesar. Write his speech, based on what you have learned about him in the play.

2. In real life, the common people of Rome rioted for three days after the burial of Caesar. As a human interest story to accompany the news report of Caesar's death, "interview" various citizens from Rome and report on the mood of the city.

3. Look back at your answer to #2 in Literary Elements. Write a short essay explaining the effectiveness of Antony's funeral oration. Why do you think the crowd of Romans responded emotionally to his speech and not to Brutus'?

Julius Caesar ACT IV

Within the Tent (Brutus sees Caesar's ghost.) Edward Austin Abbey, 1905.

"...thou shalt see me at Philippi."

Setting the Scene

JULIUS CAESAR

Act IV, scene i *or* Three-Way Split

Critical Query: What do you think the future of the triumvirate will be?

The More You Know: Caesar's Will

Remember in Act III when Antony wooed the crowd with the contents of Caesar's will? There was one provision that he conveniently forgot to mention. Antony was one of Caesar's staunchest supporters and was probably expecting to be well rewarded in his will. He was in for a big surprise! Perhaps Caesar knew how shallow and untrustworthy Antony actually was, because instead of leaving much to him, Caesar posthumously adopted his nephew Octavius and made him heir to his fortune.

Who's Who? Octavius

Octavius was a sickly 19-year-old when he inherited his uncle's treasure. Being Caesar's heir gave him the right to be part of the triumvirate that ruled after Caesar's death. One of the three, Lepidus, is treated with scorn by Antony, who also underestimated Octavius. In 31 B.C., Octavius defeated Antony in the battle of Actium. In 27 B.C. he became Rome's first emperor, Augustus.

From the Prop Box

- Papers
- Large pin to "prick" the names on a list

In Character: Antony

At the end of this scene, it's Antony's turn to sit in the hot seat. The actor(s) who have played him must answer questions in character. First, ask questions as students; then try asking questions in persona. What does Antony really think about various characters in the play? What about his reputation as a party animal? Where did he get his public speaking skills? What does he think the future will hold for him?

Warm-Up Improv

You and two friends decide to go to a concert together. Since it is a very popular event and expected to sell out, the three of you take turns waiting in line overnight. The next morning, you and one of your friends reach the box office window only to learn that there are only two tickets left. Neither you nor the friend in line with you wants to give up a ticket. How do you handle your other friend?

Classroom Set Design

Members of both forums watch silently as the members of the triumvirate discuss their plans. The three members are seated at a table or desk in the center of the playing area.

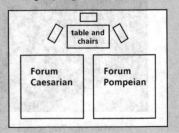

table and chairs

Forum Caesarian

Forum Pompeian

The ruling triumvirate, Antony, Octavius, and Lepidus have met at Antony's house in Rome, where they are selecting the names of Roman citizens who are to be accused of treason and put to death.

Scene i. Rome. Antony's House

❋ *[Enter* ANTONY, OCTAVIUS, *and* LEPIDUS.*]*

ANTONY. These many, then, shall die; their names are prick'd.

1 prick'd: marked by putting a pin prick through paper

OCTAVIUS. Your brother too must die. Consent you, Lepidus?

LEPIDUS. I do consent.

OCTAVIUS.   Prick him down, Antony.

LEPIDUS. Upon condition Publius shall not live,
Who is your sister's son, Mark Antony.   5

Antony, Octavius, and Lepidus (the triumvirate) decide which potential enemies must die.

❋ **Marked for Death** In Scene i of Act IV, Antony, Octavius, and Lepidus mark many people for death—including some of their own relatives. This scene was cut from all productions of the play for many years. Perhaps audiences felt queasy at seeing Rome's supposedly noble leaders cold-bloodedly planning a reign of terror.

Lepidus is sent for Caesar's will. After using it to win over the commoners, Antony is now looking for ways to avoid paying them their share. After Lepidus leaves, Antony calls Lepidus foolish, comparing him first to a pack mule and then to a horse that he has trained, used, and put out to pasture.

ANTONY. He shall not live; look, with a spot I damn him.
    But, Lepidus, go you to Caesar's house;
    Fetch the will hither, and we shall determine
    How to cut off some charge in legacies.

LEPIDUS. What, shall I find you here?   10

OCTAVIUS. Or here, or at the Capitol.

[Exit LEPIDUS.]

ANTONY. This is a slight, unmeritable man,
    Meet to be sent on errands. Is it fit,
 ✷ The threefold world divided, he should stand
    One of the three to share it?

OCTAVIUS.   So you thought him   15
    And took his voice who should be prick'd to die
    In our black sentence and proscription.

ANTONY. Octavius, I have seen more days than you,
    And, though we lay these honours on this man
    To ease ourselves of divers sland'rous loads,   20
    He shall but bear them as the ass bears gold,
    To groan and sweat under the business,
    Either led or driven, as we point the way;
    And having brought our treasure where we will,

6 with a spot I damn him: with a pin prick I condemn him

8 will: Caesar's legal will

9 cut off ... legacies: eliminate some of the items promised to people in Caesar's will

11 Or here, or: Either here or

13-15 Is it ... share it: Is it right that if the Roman world is divided into three parts (Europe, Asia, Africa) he should be one of the three to rule it?

16 voice: opinion on

17 black sentence and proscription: death sentence and condemned list

PERSONA JOURNAL

Has anyone close to you been killed since Caesar's death? How? Under what circumstances?

20 To ease ... loads: In order to lighten our burdens of blame

---

✷ **Three's a Crowd** Antony, Octavius, and Lepidus briefly controlled the Roman world as a *triumvirate*—that is, a ruling body of three men. But as this scene foreshadows, the triumvirate was quarrelsome and short-lived. War broke out between Antony and the other two leaders—a topic of Shakespeare's later play, *Antony and Cleopatra*. Eventually, Octavius emerged as Rome's first emperor. Because he was Julius Caesar's great-nephew, he came to be known as Caesar Augustus.

Antony continues his unflattering comments about Lepidus. Antony and Octavius soon turn their attention to the news that Cassius and Brutus are raising an army. They resolve to raise an army as well.

Then take we down his load and turn him off   25
(Like to the empty ass) to shake his ears
And graze in commons.

OCTAVIUS.   You may do your will,
But he's a tried and valiant soldier.

ANTONY. So is my horse, Octavius, and for that
I do appoint him store of provender.   30
It is a creature that I teach to fight,
To wind, to stop, to run directly on,
His corporal motion govern'd by my spirit;
And, in some taste, is Lepidus but so.
He must be taught, and train'd, and bid go forth—   35
A barren-spirited fellow, one that feeds
On objects, arts, and imitations
Which, out of use and stal'd by other men,
Begin his fashion. Do not talk of him
But as a property. And now, Octavius,   40
Listen great things. Brutus and Cassius
Are levying powers. We must straight make head.
Therefore let our alliance be combin'd,
Our best friends made, our means stretch'd;
And let us presently go sit in council   45
How covert matters may be best disclos'd
And open perils surest answerèd.

✱ OCTAVIUS. Let us do so, for we are at the stake
And bay'd about with many enemies,
And some that smile have in their hearts, I fear,   50
Millions of mischiefs.

[Exeunt.]

26 empty: unburdened

27 in commons: on public lands

30 I do appoint ... provender: I will provide him with a supply of food.

32 wind: turn

33 corporal motion govern'd: bodily movement controlled

34 taste: degree

36 barren-spirited: dull, uncreative

❓ According to Antony, what function does Lepidus perform for the triumvirate?

38 out of ... men: once they are no longer of value to others

40 property: tool

41 Listen great things: Listen to important things

42 straight make head: immediately raise an army

44 made: gathered; **means stretch'd:** resources utilized

❓ Do you think Lepidus suspects that Antony has such a low opinion of him?

46 covert: secret; **disclos'd:** discovered

47 open perils surest answered: obvious dangers successfully handled

48–49 at the ... about: reference to the bear in bear-baiting, where the bear is tied to a stake and then attacked by dogs

❓ How has Antony changed since the beginning of the play?

LOYALTY CHECK

If you wish to change loyalties at this point, turn your insignia over now.

✱ **Bear Facts** Octavius is referring to bear-baiting, a cruel but popular sport in Shakespeare's time. In it, a bear was tied to a stake and attacked by vicious dogs. A "bear garden" near the Globe Theatre gave Shakespeare's company considerable competition, possibly prompting the playwright to add gratuitous violence to his plays. Octavius' line is echoed in Shakespeare's later play, *Macbeth*, when its hero exclaims, "They have tied me to a stake. I cannot fly,/But, bear-like, I must fight the course."

Setting the Scene

JULIUS CAESAR

Act IV, Scenes ii and iii *or* With Friends Like These, Who Needs Enemies?

Critical Query: Which camp—that of the triumvirate or that of Brutus and Cassius—seems better prepared for battle?

Special Effects

- Drumbeats
- Music from stringed instrument (lute)

In Character: Cassius

It's Cassius' turn for the hot seat. What do you want to know about him? Why does he keep letting Brutus win every argument? What does he think of Brutus' self-professed honor and nobility? How would he compare himself to Brutus? To Caesar?

Famous Quotes from Scene iii

- An itching palm
- There is a tide in the affairs of men,/which, taken at the flood, leads on to fortune. . .
- Nature must obey necessity. . .

Classroom Set Design

Again the room is divided in two, but now instead of forums, there are army camps. Play Scene ii at the back of the classroom and have the front of the room serve as Brutus' tent where Scene iii takes place. Use a student desk for a small table where wine and candles will be set. One or two chairs will also be needed.

	Desk
table and chairs	
Camp Caesarian	Camp Pompeian

On Location: Sardis and Phillipi

Sardis was the capital of the ancient country of Lydia in what is now Turkey. Phillipi is located in the northwestern corner of Greece. As he often does in this play, Shakespeare has collapsed time for dramatic purpose. Though it seems that the battle at Phillipi occurs the day after this scene, Sardis and Phillipi are actually two hundred miles apart.

Warm-Up Improv

You have not seen your friend in months. You have heard that he/she has been talking about you to others and it was not flattering. You assume that what you have heard is true, so when you see your friend again you confront him/her.

From the Prop Box

- Dagger for Cassius
- Wine goblets and wine bottle
- Candlesticks and candles
- Letters
- Gown for Brutus with book in pocket

At his camp near Sardis, Brutus waits for Cassius to arrive. There have been disagreements between the two, and their friendship has cooled.

Act IV   Scene ii

Scene ii. The Camp Near Sardis, before the Tent of Brutus

[Drum. Enter BRUTUS, LUCILIUS, (LUCIUS), *and the army.* TITINIUS *and* PINDARUS *meet them.]*

BRUTUS. Stand ho!

LUCILIUS. Give the word, ho, and stand!

BRUTUS. What now, Lucilius, is Cassius near?

LUCILIUS. He is at hand, and Pindarus is come
    To do you salutation from his master.   5

BRUTUS. He greets me well.—Your master, Pindarus,
    In his own change or by ill officers,
    Hath given me some worthy cause to wish
    Things done undone, but if he be at hand
    I shall be satisfied.

PINDARUS.   I do not doubt   10
    But that my noble master will appear
    Such as he is, full of regard and honour.

BRUTUS. He is not doubted. A word, Lucilius,

*[*BRUTUS *and* LUCILIUS *walk aside.]*

    How he receiv'd you. Let me be resolv'd.

LUCILIUS. With courtesy and with respect enough,   15
    But not with such familiar instances,
    Nor with such free and friendly conference
    As he hath us'd of old.

PERSONA JOURNAL

What have you been doing in camp as you wait for the conflict to begin?

1 ho: there

2 word: command

5 master: meaning Cassius

6 He greets me well: Cassius has sent a worthy messenger

7 In his ... officers: Either by a change in his own feelings for me or by listening to bad advice from his officers

8 worthy: justifiable

10 be satisfied: receive an explanation from him

12 regard: respect

14 resolv'd: fully informed

16 familiar instances: congenial signs

17 conference: conversation

Brutus reflects on the signs indicating that a relationship has soured. Cassius enters and starts to explain that Brutus has judged him unfairly.

BRUTUS.   Thou hast describ'd
　　A hot friend cooling. Ever note, Lucilius,
　　When love begins to sicken and decay   20
　　It useth an enforcèd ceremony.
　　There are no tricks in plain and simple faith;
✱　But hollow men, like horses hot at hand,
　　Make gallant show and promise of their mettle,

[Low march within.]

　　But when they should endure the bloody spur,   25
　　They fall their crests and, like deceitful jades,
　　Sink in the trial. Comes his army on?

LUCILIUS. They mean this night in Sardis to be quarter'd.
　　The greater part, the horse in general,
　　Are come with Cassius.

[Enter CASSIUS *and his powers.]*

BRUTUS.   Hark, he is arrived.   30
　　March gently on to meet him.

CASSIUS. Stand ho!

BRUTUS. Stand ho! Speak the word along.

FIRST SOLDIER. Stand!

SECOND SOLDIER. Stand!   35

THIRD SOLDIER. Stand!

CASSIUS. Most noble brother, you have done me wrong.

---

21 enforcèd ceremony: forced politeness

23–27 But hollow men ... trial: Insincere men are like horses who at first appear high-spirited, but then lower their heads like nags and fail when actually put to the test.

28 quarter'd: camped

29 horse in general: the cavalry

37 brother: brother-in-law or dear friend

✱　**"But hollow men, like horses hot at hand. . ."** The influence of Shakespeare's language and imagery reaches far and wide. T.S. Eliot, one of the 20th century's most important poets, was inspired by Brutus' remark to write his 1925 poem "The Hollow Men." "We are the hollow men," Eliot's poem begins. "We are the stuffed men/Leaning together/Headpiece filled with straw." This great poem was quoted by Marlon Brando's character in the 1979 movie *Apocalypse Now*.

Cassius and Brutus begin to argue, but stop when Brutus points out that their armies should not see them squabbling. The soldiers are moved away from Brutus' tent, and the two leaders enter to continue their conversation.

BRUTUS. Judge me, you gods! Wrong I mine enemies?
      And if not so, how should I wrong a brother?

CASSIUS. Brutus, this sober form of yours hides wrongs,   40
      And when you do them—

BRUTUS.   Cassius, be content.
      Speak your griefs softly. I do know you well.
      Before the eyes of both our armies here
      (Which should perceive nothing but love from us),
      Let us not wrangle. Bid them move away;   45
      Then in my tent, Cassius, enlarge your griefs,
      And I will give you audience.

CASSIUS.   Pindarus,
      Bid our commanders lead their charges off
      A little from this ground.

BRUTUS. Lucius, do you the like, and let no man   50
      Come to our tent till we have done our conference.
      Let Lucilius and Titinius guard our door.

✱ *[Exeunt all but* BRUTUS *and* CASSIUS.*]*

40 this sober form of yours: this formal, dignified manner

❓ How might Brutus speak as he cuts Cassius off and tries to keep others from overhearing?

41 content: calm

42 griefs: complaints

46 enlarge: express

48 charges: troops

✱ **Breaking Up** In today's editions, Shakespeare's plays are divided into scenes and acts. But Shakespeare himself didn't make such divisions. To him, a play was a continuous flow of action. Act and scene breaks were added by later editors. In Shakespeare's original production, all characters except Brutus and Cassius simply exited at the end of "Scene ii," then Brutus and Cassius may have moved to a different part of the stage. This was all that was needed to indicate a new location—inside Brutus' tent.

Cassius is angry and confrontational because Brutus ignored his request to pardon a friend for taking bribes. Brutus accuses Cassius of taking bribes himself and of tarnishing their names and their cause.

Scene iii. The Camp near Sardis, within the Tent of Brutus

CASSIUS. That you have wrong'd me doth appear in this:
    You have condemn'd and noted Lucius Pella
    For taking bribes here of the Sardians,
    Wherein my letters, praying on his side
    Because I knew the man, was slighted off.   5

BRUTUS. You wrong'd yourself to write in such a case.

CASSIUS. In such a time as this it is not meet
    That every nice offense should bear his comment.

BRUTUS. Let me tell you, Cassius, you yourself
    Are much condemn'd to have an itching palm,   10
    To sell and mart your offices for gold
    To undeservers.

CASSIUS.   I an itching palm?
    You know that you are Brutus that speaks this,
    Or, by the gods, this speech were else your last.

BRUTUS. The name of Cassius honours this corruption,   15
    And chastisement doth therefore hide his head.

CASSIUS. Chatisement?

BRUTUS. Remember March; the ides of March remember.
    Did not great Julius bleed for justice' sake?

? Now that Brutus and Cassius are alone, will Cassius express himself differently? How?

2 noted: publicly disgraced

4 praying: asking for leniency

5 slighted off: disregarded with contempt

7 meet: proper

8 nice: trivial; **bear his comment:** be punished

10 much condemn'd … palm: often accused of taking bribes

11 mart your offices: use your good name

15 honours: protects

16 chastisement doth … head: therefore these crimes escape punishment

---

TALES FROM THE STAGE
Caesar = Castro

As Orson Welles demonstrated in 1937, *Julius Caesar* can be updated to fit almost any political situation involving tyranny and rebellion. In 1986, a Miami production of Shakespeare's play portrayed Caesar as a Castro-like leader of a Latin-American Communist regime. Audiences rose to their feet and cheered when he was assassinated.

What villain touch'd his body that did stab   20
And not for justice? What, shall one of us
That struck the foremost man of all this world
But for supporting robbers, shall we now
Contaminate our fingers with base bribes
And sell the mighty space of our large honours   25
For so much trash as may be graspèd thus?
I had rather be a dog, and bay the moon
Than such a Roman.

CASSIUS.   Brutus, bait not me.
I'll not endure it. You forget yourself
To hedge me in. I am a soldier, I,   30
Older in practice, abler than yourself
To make conditions.

BRUTUS.   Go to! You are not, Cassius.

CASSIUS. I am.

BRUTUS. I say you are not.

? Do you think Cassius stabbed Caesar for the sake of justice? Explain.

23 But for: Because he was

25 sell the … honours: use our integrity as a front for influence-peddling

26 trash: worthless money

27 bay: howl at

28 bait: attack

30 hedge me in: back me into a corner

31 Older in practice: More experienced

32 make conditions: manage things

Brutus (Martin Sheen) accuses Cassius (Edward Herrmann) of theft and bribery. New York Shakespeare Festival, 1988.

Brutus tells Cassius that he will publicly ridicule him. Each man tells the other that he has overstepped the boundaries of friendship. Brutus declares that he is the stronger one because his integrity is still intact.

CASSIUS. Urge me no more. I shall forget myself.   35
Have mind upon your health. Tempt me no farther.

BRUTUS. Away, slight man!

CASSIUS. Is't possible?

BRUTUS.   Hear me, for I will speak.
Must I give way and room to your rash choler?
Shall I be frighted when a madman stares?   40

CASSIUS. O ye gods, ye gods, must I endure all this?

BRUTUS. All this? Ay, more. Fret till your proud heart break.
Go show your slaves how choleric you are
And make your bondmen tremble. Must I budge?
Must I observe you? Must I stand and crouch   45
Under your testy humour? By the gods,
You shall digest the venom of your spleen
Though it do split you. For, from this day forth,
I'll use you for my mirth, yea, for my laughter,
When you are waspish.

CASSIUS.   Is it come to this?   50

BRUTUS. You say you are a better solider.
Let it appear so, make your vaunting true,
And it shall please me well. For mine own part,
I shall be glad to learn of noble men.

CASSIUS. You wrong me every way, you wrong me, Brutus.   55
I said an elder solider, not a better.
Did I say "better"?

35 **Urge:** Provoke

37 **slight:** worthless

39 **give way ... choler:** put up with and make allowances for your bad temper?

44 **bondmen:** slaves
45 **crouch:** bow
46 **humour:** disposition
47 **digest the venom of your spleen:** keep your anger to yourself

49 **mirth:** jokes

50 **waspish:** angry as a wasp

52 **vaunting:** boasts

54 **of:** from

An Actor's Dream This scene between Cassius and Brutus is one of the most highly praised passages in the play. Here, Shakespeare vividly and plausibly presents the two men's quarrel and reconciliation. The scene serves as an important dramatic function in increasing the audience's sympathy for Brutus—and even for the less-than-scrupulous Cassius. Also, it is a favorite showpiece for two actors, allowing them to run a range of emotions including rage, sorrow, pity, and affection.

Brutus reveals that he is angry with Cassius because Cassius denied Brutus' request for money to pay his troops. Cassius replies that there was a misunderstanding about the funds. Each accuses the other of not being a true friend.

BRUTUS.   If you did, I care not.

CASSIUS. When Caesar liv'd, he durst not thus have mov'd me.

BRUTUS. Peace, peace! You durst not so have tempted him.

CASSIUS. I durst not?   60

BRUTUS. No.

CASSIUS. What, durst not tempt him?

BRUTUS.   For your life you durst not.

CASSIUS. Do not presume too much upon my love.
    I may do that I shall be sorry for.

64 **that:** that which

BRUTUS. You have done that you should be sorry for.   65
    There is no terror, Cassius, in your threats,
✱ For I am arm'd so strong in honesty
    That they pass by me as the idle wind,
    Which I respect not. I did send to you
    For certain sums of gold, which you denied me,   70
    For I can raise no money by vile means.
    By heaven, I had rather coin my heart
    And drop my blood for drachmas than to wring
    From the hard hands of peasants their vile trash
    By any indirection. I did send   75
    To you for gold to pay my legions,
    Which you denied me. Was that done like Cassius?
    Should I have answered Caius Cassius so?
    When Marcus Brutus grows so covetous
    To lock such rascal counters from his friends,   80
    Be ready, gods, with all your thunderbolts;
    Dash him to pieces!

67 **honesty:** honor or integrity

73 **drachmas:** unit of money

74 **trash:** money

75 **indirection:** crooked means

76 **legions:** soldiers

79–80 **covetous/To ... counters:** miserly/as to keep away such worthless coins

✱ **Not So Perfect After All** Here we learn that Brutus' idealism has its limits. He has just accused Cassius of corruption—of selling ranks and offices for gold. But Brutus is also angry at Cassius for not *sharing* his ill-gotten gains with him—"For I can raise no money by vile means," he says, rather piously. Of course, Brutus doesn't want this money for himself but to help finance the war. Even so, this moment reveals a hint of hypocrisy in Brutus' character.

Cassius dramatically declares that he would rather not live now that he has angered someone he loves, honors, and respects.

Act IV   Scene iii

CASSIUS.   I denied you not.

BRUTUS. You did.

CASSIUS. I did not. He was but a fool that brought
My answer back. Brutus hath riv'd my heart.   85
A friend should bear his friend's infirmities,
But Brutus makes mine greater than they are.

BRUTUS. I do not, till you practice them on me.

CASSIUS. You love me not.

BRUTUS.   I do not like your faults.

CASSIUS. A friendly eye could never see such faults.   90

BRUTUS. A flatterer's would not, though they do appear
As huge as high Olympus.

CASSIUS. Come, Antony, and young Octavius, come!
Revenge yourselves alone on Cassius,
For Cassius is aweary of the world—   95
Hated by one he loves, brav'd by his brother,
Check'd like a bondman, all his faults observ'd,
Set in a notebook, learn'd, and conn'd by rote
To cast into my teeth. O, I could weep
My spirit from mine eyes! There is my dagger,   100

✱ *[Offering his dagger to BRUTUS.]*

And here my naked breast; within, a heart
Dearer than Pluto's mine, richer than gold.
If that thou be'st a Roman, take it forth.
I that denied thee gold will give my heart.
Strike as thou didst at Caesar, for I know   105
When thou didst hate him worst, thou lov'dst him better
Than ever thou lov'dst Cassius.

? What do you think of Brutus' condemning Cassius for raising money unjustly and then becoming angry because Cassius would not share his ill-gotten gains?

85 riv'd: broken

96 brav'd: defied

97 Check'd like a bondman: Rebuked like a slave

98 conn'd by rote: memorized

99 cast into my teeth: throw into my face

102 Dearer than Pluto's mine: Of greater value than all of Pluto's gold and silver mines. Pluto was the god of the underworld and therefore of underground mines.

103 that thou be'st: you really are

✱ **Scenic Description** You've probably learned that a good story (or play) has a rising action (or conflict) leading to a climax, followed by a falling action (or resolution). The same is true of a well-written scene like this one. The quarrel between Brutus and Cassius reaches its emotional climax when Cassius offers Brutus his dagger and appeals to his love. Brutus is deeply affected by this moment, and the rest of their dialogue is falling action, revealing their deepening friendship.

Cassius and Brutus at Brutus' tent in the camp near Sardis

Cassius confesses that his bad temper is an embarrassment. Brutus takes responsibility for the argument as well, and the two apologize to each other.

BRUTUS.   Sheathe your dagger.
Be angry when you will, it shall have scope.
Do what you will, dishonour shall be humour.
O Cassius, you are yokèd with a lamb   110
That carries anger as the flint bears fire,
Who, much enforcèd, shows a hasty spark
And straight is cold again.

CASSIUS.   Hath Cassius liv'd
To be but mirth and laughter to his Brutus
When grief and blood ill-temper'd vexeth him?   115

BRUTUS. When I spoke that, I was ill-temper'd too.

CASSIUS. Do you confess so much? Give me your hand.

BRUTUS. And my heart too.

[They clasp hands.]

CASSIUS.   O Brutus!

BRUTUS.   What's the matter?

CASSIUS. Have not you love enough to bear with me
When that rash humour which my mother gave me   120
Makes me forgetful?

BRUTUS.   Yes, Cassius, and from henceforth
When you are over-earnest with your Brutus,
He'll think your mother chides, and leave you so.

[Enter a POET, followed by LUCILIUS, TITINIUS, and LUCIUS.]

POET. Let me go in to see the Generals.
There is some grudge between 'em; 'tis not meet   125
They be alone.

LUCILIUS.   You shall not come to them.

❓ Do you think the conspirators feel as positive about the assassination of Caesar as they once did? Why or why not?

107 Sheathe: Put away

108 it shall have scope: you shall have the freedom to do so

109 dishonour shall be humour: I will disregard your insults as merely displays of your bad temper

110 yokèd: partnered

112 much enforcèd: when struck

113 straight: immediately

114 mirth: a joke

115 blood ill-temper'd: unbalanced emotion

120 that rash humour which my mother gave me: the angry temper I inherited from my mother

122 are over-earnest with your Brutus: take me too seriously

❓ Who does Cassius blame for his bad behavior?

125 meet: fitting

Suddenly, a poet forces his way into the tent. He manages to rebuke both men for quarreling before he is forced to leave. Brutus and Cassius call for wine and order their troops to settle in for the night.

POET. Nothing but death shall stay me.

CASSIUS. How now, what's the matter?

POET. For shame, you generals, what do you mean?
    Love and be friends as two such men should be,   130
    For I have seen more years, I'm sure, than ye.

✳ **CASSIUS.** Ha, ha, how vilely doth this cynic rhyme!

BRUTUS. Get you hence, sirrah! Saucy fellow, hence!

CASSIUS. Bear with him, Brutus. 'Tis his fashion.

BRUTUS. I'll know his humour when he knows his time.   135
    What should the wars do with these jigging fools?—
    Companion, hence!

CASSIUS.   Away, away, be gone!

[Exit POET.]

BRUTUS. Lucilius and Titinius, bid the commanders
    Prepare to lodge their companies tonight.

CASSIUS. And come yourselves, and bring Messala with you   140
    Immediately to us.

[Exeunt LUCILIUS and TITINIUS.]

BRUTUS.   Lucius, a bowl of wine.

[Exit LUCIUS.]

CASSIUS. I did not think you could have been so angry.

BRUTUS. O Cassius, I am sick of many griefs.

---

132 cynic: cynic philosopher or rude, boorish fellow

133 Saucy: Insolent

135 I'll know ... time: I'll put up with his behavior when he learns the proper time and place to display it.

136 jigging: rhyming

137 Companion: Fellow

LOYALTY CHECK

If you wish to change sides, turn your insignia over now.

❓ Directors sometimes cut the part of the poet. Would you? Why might Shakespeare have included him?

✳ **Cynicism** Today, we think of a cynic as someone who takes a sour view of just about everything. But in the ancient world, cynicism was a philosophy that rejected social institutions like the family, advocated unconventional behavior, and demanded an extremely simple lifestyle. The most famous of all cynics was the Greek Diogenes (c. 412–323 B.C.). He was said to have begged for his living, slept in a tub, and carried a lamp even by day as he searched in vain for a truly honest man.

Brutus informs Cassius that Portia is dead. Cassius is shocked and instantly realizes why Brutus has been so unlike himself. Brutus explains that Portia became depressed and committed suicide.

✱ CASSIUS. Of your philosophy you make no use
If you give place to accidental evils.   145

BRUTUS. No man bears sorrow better. Portia is dead.

CASSIUS. Ha? Portia?

BRUTUS. She is dead.

CASSIUS. How 'scaped I killing when I cross'd you so?
O insupportable and touching loss!   150
Upon what sickness?

BRUTUS.   Impatient of my absence,
And grief that young Octavius with Mark Antony
Have made themselves so strong—for with her death
That tidings came—with this she fell distract
And, her attendants absent, swallow'd fire.   155

CASSIUS. And died so?

BRUTUS.   Even so.

CASSIUS.   O ye immortal gods!

144 philosophy: Stoicism. Brutus was a Stoic. He believed that no change of fortune should affect a man's inner tranquillity and peace of mind.

145 give place to accidental evils: let yourself be affected by chance misfortunes

149 'scaped I killing: did I escape being killed

151 Upon: Of

151 Impatient of: Unable to bear

154 tidings: news; **fell distract:** became depressed

155 swallow'd fire: she swallowed hot coals

? What earlier action foreshadowed Portia's painful death?

PERSONA JOURNAL

How did you hear of Portia's death?

Cassius (Dennis Boutsikaris) and Brutus (Jamey Sheridan). Shakespeare in Central Park, New York, 2000.

✱ Stoicism and Platonism When Cassius mentions Brutus' philosophy, he means *Stoicism,* which taught that one should accept all of life's events—both good and bad—with calm detachment. But there's always been controversy as to whether Brutus was really Stoic. According to Plutarch's *Lives,* Brutus was instead a Platonist—one who believed that the sensory world was an illusion, and that true reality could be grasped only by reason.

Titinius and Messala arrive to discuss recent developments and to make plans. Brutus informs the group that Octavius and Mark Antony have raised an army and are on the march to Philippi. Messala has heard that Octavius, Mark Antony, and Lepidus have put to death 100 senators.

[Enter LUCIUS *with wine and tapers.]*

BRUTUS. Speak no more of her.—Give me a bowl of wine.—
    In this I bury all unkindness, Cassius.

[Drinks.]

CASSIUS. My heart is thirsty for that noble pledge.—
    Fill, Lucius, till the wine o'erswell the cup;   160
    I cannot drink too much of Brutus' love.

[Drinks.]

[Exit LUCIUS.*]*

[Enter TITINIUS *and* MESSALA.*]*

BRUTUS. Come in, Titinius. Welcome, good Messala.
    Now sit we close about this taper here,
    And call in question our necessities.

[They sit.]

CASSIUS. Portia, art thou gone?

BRUTUS.   No more, I pray you.—   165
    Messala, I have here receivèd letters
    That young Octavius and Mark Antony
    Come down upon us with a mighty power,
    Bending their expedition toward Philippi.

MESSALA. Myself have letters of the selfsame tenor.   170

BRUTUS. With what addition?

MESSALA. That by proscription and bills of outlawry,
    Octavius, Antony, and Lepidus
    Have put to death an hundred senators.

164 call in … necessities: examine what we need to do

169 Philippi: a city in Macedonia

170 letters of the selfsame tenor: letters with the same information

172 proscription and … outlawry: condemnation and legal decrees

PERSONA JOURNAL

Did you witness the deaths of any of the senators? How have these events affected you?

Brutus says he's heard that Cicero was killed by the triumvirate. Messala, thinking that he does not know, tells Brutus that his wife is dead. Brutus and Cassius discuss the pros and cons of marching to Philippi to confront Octavius' and Antony's armies. This is the plan Brutus favors.

BRUTUS. Therein our letters do not well agree.   175
    Mine speak of seventy senators that died
    By their proscriptions, Cicero being one.

CASSIUS. Cicero one?

MESSALA.   Cicero is dead,
    And by that order of proscription.
    Had you your letters from your wife, my lord?   180

BRUTUS. No, Messala.

MESSALA. Nor nothing in your letters writ of her?

BRUTUS. Nothing, Messala.

MESSALA.   That methinks is strange.

BRUTUS. Why ask you? Hear you aught of her in yours?

MESSALA. No, my lord.   185

BRUTUS. Now, as you are a Roman, tell me true.

MESSALA. Then like a Roman bear the truth I tell,
    For certain she is dead, and by strange manner.

BRUTUS. Why, farewell, Portia. We must die, Messala.
    With meditating that she must die once,   190
    I have the patience to endure it now.

MESSALA. Even so great men great losses should endure.

✱ **CASSIUS.** I have as much of this in art as you,
    But yet my nature could not bear it so.

BRUTUS. Well, to our work alive. What do you think   195
    Of marching to Philippi presently?

CASSIUS. I do not think it good.

180 **Had you your letters:** Did you receive a letter

182 **writ of:** written about

183 **That methinks:** I think that

184 **aught of:** anything about

189 **must die:** must all die
190 **With meditating:** Knowing

193 **I have … you:** I am as much a believer in Stoic strength of will as you, Brutus.
195 **alive:** that concerns the living
196 **presently:** right away

✱ **Double Trouble** Some critics think the previous lines (starting from Messala's "Had you your letters from your wife, my lord?") ought to be cut. After all, Brutus seems to learn all over again that Portia has died. Perhaps these lines were accidentally left over from an earlier draft of the play. But other critics defend this passage, claiming that hearing again of Portia's death gives Brutus yet another moment to demonstrate his Stoic calm.

Cassius wants to stay where they are and wait for Octavius and Antony to come to them. Brutus insists his plan is better and that they must seize the moment.

BRUTUS.   Your reason?

CASSIUS.   This it is:
   'Tis better that the enemy seek us;
   So shall he waste his means, weary his soldiers,
   Doing himself offense, whilst we, lying still,   200
   Are full of rest, defense, and nimbleness.

BRUTUS. Good reasons must of force give place to better.
   The people 'twixt Philippi and this ground
   Do stand but in a forc'd affection,
   For they have grudg'd us contribution.   205
   The enemy, marching along by them,
   By them shall make a fuller number up,
   Come on refresh'd, new-added, and encourag'd;
   From which advantage shall we cut him off
   If at Philippi we do face him there,   210
   These people at our back.

CASSIUS.   Hear me, good brother.—

BRUTUS. Under your pardon. You must note beside
   That we have tried the utmost of our friends,
   Our legions are brim full, our cause is ripe.
   The enemy increaseth every day;   215
   We, at the height, are ready to decline.
✱ There is a tide in the affairs of men,
   Which, taken at the flood, leads on to fortune;
   Omitted, all the voyage of their life
   Is bound in shallows and in miseries.   220
   On such a full sea are we now afloat,
   And we must take the current when it serves
   Or lose our ventures.

199 means: resources

200 offense: harm

202 of force: by necessity

203 'twixt: between

204 Do stand ... affection: Support us only because they are forced to do so

205 grudg'd us contribution: begrudged us assistance

206–207 by them/By ... up: through their lands shall increase their numbers by forcing the local people into service

208 new-added: newly reinforced

212 Under your pardon: Excuse me; **note beside:** also notice

213 tried the ... friends: demanded from our friends all that they can provide

❓ Brutus does not listen to Cassius. Why does he cut him off?

218 the flood: its highest point

219 Omitted: Not taken

220 bound in shallows: confined in shallow waters

223 our ventures: all that we have risked

❓ What are Brutus' reasons for wanting to meet the enemy at Philippi? Why does Cassius prefer to wait and let the battle come to him? Which plan would you choose?

✱ **"There is a tide in the affairs of men ..."** This is one of the most often-quoted phrases in all of Shakespeare. He may have gotten the image from the River Thames in London. Londoners living on the north bank of the Thames had to take a boat across the river to get to the Globe Theatre. This was difficult when the tide was low, for one had to wade through considerable mud getting to the boat, and then again upon reaching the other side of the river. So an outing to the Globe was best "taken at the flood."

Cassius reluctantly agrees to Brutus' plan. They will begin the march to Philippi the next morning.

Act IV   Scene iii

CASSIUS.   Then, with your will, go on;
    We'll along ourselves and meet them at Philippi.

BRUTUS. The deep of the night is crept upon our talk,   225
    And nature must obey necessity,
    Which we will niggard with a little rest.
    There is no more to say.

CASSIUS.   No more. Good night.

[They stand.]

    Early tomorrow will we rise and hence.

BRUTUS. Lucius!
[Enter LUCIUS.*]*

                    My gown.
[Exit LUCIUS.*]*

Farewell, good Messala.—   230
    Good night, Titinius.—Noble, noble Cassius,
    Good night and good repose.

CASSIUS.   O my dear brother,
    This was an ill beginning of the night.
    Never come such division 'tween our souls;
    Let it not, Brutus.

[Enter LUCIUS *with the gown.]*

BRUTUS.   Everything is well.   235

CASSIUS. Good night, my lord.

BRUTUS.   Good night, good brother.

TITINIUS, MESSALA. Good night, Lord Brutus.

BRUTUS.   Farewell every one.

[Exeunt CASSIUS, TITINIUS, *and* MESSALA.*]*

223 **with your will:** as you wish

❓ Why does Cassius give in to Brutus' wishes?

226 **necessity:** physical need

227 **niggard:** satisfy

229 **hence:** go forward

Brutus calls for Varro and Claudius to sleep in his tent. As they settle in, Brutus asks his young servant Lucius to play a song or two.

Act IV Scene iii

Give me the gown. Where is thy instrument?

LUCIUS. Here in the tent.

BRUTUS.   What, thou speak'st drowsily?
  ❋ Poor knave, I blame thee not; thou art o'erwatch'd.   240
   Call Claudius and some other of my men;
   I'll have them sleep on cushions in my tent.

LUCIUS. Varro and Claudius.

[Enter VARRO *and* CLAUDIUS.*]*

VARRO. Calls my lord?

BRUTUS. I pray you, sirs, lie in my tent and sleep.   245
   It may be I shall raise you by and by
   On business to my brother Cassius.

VARRO. So please you, we will stand and watch your pleasure.

BRUTUS. I will not have it so. Lie down, good sirs.
   It may be I shall otherwise bethink me.   250

[They lie down.]

   Look, Lucius, here's the book I sought for so.
   I put it in the pocket of my gown.

LUCIUS. I was sure your lordship did not give it me.

BRUTUS. Bear with me, good boy, I am much forgetful.
   Canst thou hold up thy heavy eyes awhile,   255
   And touch thy instrument a strain or two?

LUCIUS. Ay, my lord, an't please you.

BRUTUS.   It does, my boy.

238 instrument: probably a lute

239 thou speak'st drowsily: you sound tired

240 knave: lad; **o'erwatch'd:** exhausted from staying awake on guard duty

248 watch your pleasure: attend your wishes

250 otherwise bethink me: change my mind

251 sought for so: was searching for

256 touch: play

❋ **Brutus' Compassion** Shakespeare had a tough job on his hands in generating audience sympathy for Brutus. Aside from being the leader of a ruthless political assassination, Brutus often seems a cold, intellectual idealist. But throughout the play, Shakespeare also portrays Brutus as less concerned with himself than with other people—especially servants like Lucius and common soldiers like Varrus and Claudius. Such moments of compassion prompt us to care about Brutus, despite his flaws and limitations.

Lucius plays the lute for his master, Brutus (Orson Welles), 1937.

I trouble thee too much, but thou art willing.

LUCIUS. It is my duty, sir.

BRUTUS. I should not urge thy duty past thy might;   260
     I know young bloods look for a time of rest.

LUCIUS. I have slept, my lord, already.

BRUTUS. It was well done, and thou shalt sleep again;
     I will not hold thee long. If I do live,
     I will be good to thee.   265

[Music and a song.]

260 thy might: your strength

261 young bloods ... rest: young people need a lot of sleep

After Lucius plays a lullaby, he falls asleep. As Brutus reads, he is suddenly startled by the appearance of Caesar's ghost.

This is a sleepy tune. O murd'rous slumber.
Layest thou thy leaden mace upon my boy,
That plays thee music?—Gentle knave, good night.
I will not do thee so much wrong to wake thee.
If thou dost nod, thou break'st thy instrument.   270
I'll take it from thee and, good boy, good night.

[He moves the instrument.]

Let me see, let me see; is not the leaf turn'd down
Where I left reading? Here it is, I think.
How ill this taper burns.

❋ *[Enter the* GHOST *of Caesar.]*

            Ha! who comes here?—
I think it is the weakness of mine eyes   275
That shapes this monstrous apparition.

266 murd'rous slumber: sleep as an image of death

267 Layest thou ... mace: Do you lay your heavy staff

272 leaf: page

274 ill: dimly

276 apparition: ghost

❓ As director, what would you do about the ghost? Would it be an actor or just a figment of Brutus' imagination?

Brutus is visited by the spirit of Julius Caesar (whom he helped to assassinate) the night before the battle of Philippi (in which he was defeated).

❋ **Great Caesar's Ghost!** According to Plutarch's *Lives*, the apparition that appeared to Brutus at Sardis wasn't Caesar's ghost, but Brutus' "ill angel." Perhaps Shakespeare made this change in order to remind Brutus (and us) that the true spirit of Caesar—the principle of power and majesty in the world—can never be killed. Indeed, the "Ghost of Caesar," seems to haunt the entire play after his death. This may help explain why Shakespeare called his play *Julius Caesar* and not *Brutus*.

The ghost has come to tell Brutus that they will meet again in Philippi. The apparition vanishes and Brutus quickly wakens Lucius, Varro, and Claudius.

It comes upon me.—Art thou any thing?
Art thou some god, some angel, or some devil,
That mak'st my blood cold and my hair to stare?
Speak to me what thou art.   280

GHOST. Thy evil spirit, Brutus.

BRUTUS.   Why com'st thou?

GHOST. To tell thee thou shalt see me at Philippi.

BRUTUS. Well, then I shall see thee again?

GHOST. Ay, at Philippi.

BRUTUS. Why, I will see thee at Philippi then.   285

[GHOST *exits.*]

Now I have taken heart, thou vanishest.
Ill spirit, I would hold more talk with thee.—
Boy, Lucius! Varro! Claudius, sirs, awake!
Claudius!

LUCIUS. The strings, my lord, are false.

BRUTUS. He thinks he still is at his instrument.   290
Lucius, awake!

LUCIUS. My lord?

BRUTUS. Didst thou dream, Lucius, that thou so criedst out?

LUCIUS. My lord, I do not know that I did cry.

BRUTUS. Yes, that thou didst. Didst thou see anything?   295

LUCIUS. Nothing, my lord.

277 upon: toward

279 stare: stand on end

❓ What do you think the ghost means when it says "thou shalt see me at Philippi"?

❓ What is Brutus' attitude about the ghost?

286 taken heart: gotten my courage back

289 false: out of tune

Brutus orders Varro and Claudius to tell Cassius to begin his march early the next morning and that he will follow with his troops.

Act IV   Scene iii

BRUTUS. Sleep again, Lucius.—Sirrah Claudius!
   [To VARRO*]* Fellow thou, awake!

[They rise up.]

VARRO. My lord?

CLAUDIUS. My lord?

BRUTUS. Why did you so cry out, sirs, in your sleep?

BOTH. Did we, my lord?   300

BRUTUS.   Ay. Saw you anything?

VARRO. No, my lord, I saw nothing.

CLAUDIUS.   Nor I, my lord.

BRUTUS. Go and commend me to my brother Cassius.
   Bid him set on his powers betimes before,   305
   And we will follow.

BOTH.   It shall be done, my lord.

[Exeunt.]

297 Sirrah: My good man

304 commend me: pay my respects

305 set on ... before: advance his army early this morning before mine

PERSONA JOURNAL

How did you spend this night?

Reacting to Act IV

Analysis

1. What is your opinion of Lepidus in the first scene of this act?

2. Why do you think Cassius and Brutus quarrel?

3. What effect would you say is gained by the revelation of Portia's death?

4. If Brutus were able to go back in time and decide all over again whether to participate in the conspiracy, what do you think he would do? Why?

5. How has Antony changed since he delivered the funeral oration? Think about how his actions, words, and goals are different. Look in Act IV for specific examples that back up your views.

6. How does the triumvirate compare to the conspirators?

7. What do you think will happen in Act V, the final act of the play?

Literary Elements

1. A **tragedy** is a serious work of literature that narrates the events leading to the downfall of a **tragic hero**, who displays noble qualities but also has a **tragic flaw** or fatal character weakness. At this point in the play, who seems closest to the definition of a tragic hero?

2. Study the **dialogue** in Scene iii between Brutus and Cassius regarding Portia's death (lines 146–161). What does each man's reaction say about his character?

3. A **metaphor** is a figure of speech that makes a comparison between things that are not truly alike. An **extended metaphor** is a complex comparison that goes on for several lines. Explain the extended metaphor on page 151 involving the sea.

Writing

1. In Scene i, Antony compares Lepidus to two animals. Suggest animals that remind you of Caesar, Brutus, and Antony. Give one or two reasons for each of your choices.

2. Write up a set of charges that the triumvirate might use against one of the Roman citizens on their list.

3. Write Portia's goodbye letter to Brutus. Write that letter utilizing the language of Shakespeare.

4. Choose a quotation from one of the scenes in Act IV that you feel best characterizes that scene. In a paragraph, discuss why you think this quote is significant and effective at conveying the events or emotions of the scene.

Julius Caesar ACT V

Brutus, Ivan Kyncl, London

"Caesar, now be still. I kill'd not thee with half so good a will."

Setting the Scene

JULIUS CAESAR

Act V, Scene i *or* Face to Face

Critical Query: What is the mood of the officers in both camps?

Behind the Scene: Stage Combat

While there is no actual combat suggested in the stage directions of the play, you may wish to add some for this and the following scenes. Any such plans will require extra preparation for those involved. Detailed choreography and practice are necessary for combat scenes to be effective and safe.

- Actors should decide what type of fight is best suited for the scene.

- Plan each part of the fight step by step and move by move.

- Remember to practice falls as well as fighting. It may be easier to divide the fight into segments, practicing each segment until all parties are confident of their moves.

- Most importantly, as you plan and rehearse, rule number one is safety. No one should be hurt in a stage fight.

Classroom Set Design

Two army camps are pushed to the back of room to leave a larger playing area. (This will be the setup for the rest of the play.) Opposing forces enter from opposites sides of the room and meet at center stage.

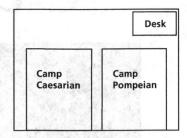

Time Capsule: Slaves

On page 166, lines 106-108, Cassius asks Brutus if he would allow himself to be led through the streets of Rome. He is referring to the custom of those captured in battle being sent back to Rome to be sold as slaves. Once a slave, you were a slave for life unless you were freed by a kind master.

Special Effects

- Drumbeats
- Trumpet call to arms

On Location: Battle Plans

As director, make a diagram(s) of the battlefield and plot the action of the armies in this scene using Xs and Os, just as you might diagram a play in sports. You may need several pages. Remember where the audience is and make sure that the principal actors can be seen. For more detailed information about the battle, read Plutarch's description in *Lives of the Noble Greeks and Romans*.

Warm-Up Improv

It's an important game with your biggest rivals. You and your team members meet to shake hands with the visitors before the competition. Some grandstanding and trash talking occurs. (Your insults must be creative. Please, no objectionable language!)

Octavius and Antony have brought their armies to a position near Philippi. They are discussing the grand posturing of Cassius' and Brutus' armies when a messenger arrives to tell them that an attack is imminent. Antony orders Octavius to take the left side of the battlefield. Octavius refuses.

* Scene i. Near Philippi

[Enter OCTAVIUS, ANTONY, and their army.]

OCTAVIUS. Now, Antony, our hopes are answerèd.
    You said the enemy would not come down
    But keep the hills and upper regions.
    It proves not so; their battles are at hand.
    They mean to warn us at Philippi here,   5
    Answering before we do demand of them.

ANTONY. Tut, I am in their bosoms, and I know
    Wherefore they do it. They could be content
    To visit other places, and come down
    With fearful bravery, thinking by this face   10
    To fasten in our thoughts that they have courage.
    But 'tis not so.

[Enter a MESSENGER.]

MESSENGER.   Prepare you, generals.
    The enemy comes on in gallant show.
    Their bloody sign of battle is hung out,
    And something to be done immediately.   15

ANTONY. Octavius, lead your battle softly on
    Upon the left hand of the even field

OCTAVIUS. Upon the right hand, I; keep thou the left.

ANTONY. Why do you cross me in this exigent?

PERSONA ACTION

Those personas currently loyal to Antony and Octavius enter with them.

PERSONA JOURNAL

The day of the battle has arrived. What are your thoughts and concerns?

3 keep: keep to

4 battles: armies

5 warn: challenge

7 am in their bosoms: have spies among them

8 Wherefore: Why

8–11 They could … courage: They would prefer (**be content**) to be in another place, and descend upon (**come down**) us with a brave show of force (**fearful bravery**), thinking that by this tactic (**face**) they will convince us (**fasten in our thoughts**) that they have great courage.

13 gallant show: splendid display

14 sign: flag

15 something: a response is needed

16 softly: slowly

19 cross: contradict; **exigent:** critical moment

? Why do you think Octavius defies Antony's instructions?

* **Time Warp** Shakespeare again plays tricks with both geography and fact to compress the action of his play. Brutus and Cassius arrived in Sardis in the spring of 42 B.C.; their battle against Antony at Philippi didn't take place until autumn the same year; but Shakespeare makes these two events seem to happen one right after the other.

Octavius makes it clear that he is in charge of his armies and does not take orders from Antony. The opposing generals, Brutus and Cassius along with Antony and Octavius, meet before the battle to talk.

OCTAVIUS. I do not cross you; but I will do so.   20

[March.]

[Drum. Enter BRUTUS, CASSIUS, *and their army, including* LUCILIUS, TITINIUS, MESSALA, *and others.]*

BRUTUS. They stand and would have parley.

CASSIUS. Stand fast, Titinius. We must out and talk.

OCTAVIUS. Mark Antony, shall we give sign of battle?

ANTONY. No, Caesar, we will answer on their charge.
      Mark forth. The Generals would have some words.   25

OCTAVIUS.

[To his OFFICERS.*]*

      Stir not until the signal.

[The GENERALS *step forward.]*

A solemn conversation between Cassius and Brutus just before the battle. Mankiewicz film, 1953

20 so: as I please

PERSONA ACTION

Personas loyal to Brutus and Cassius enter with them.

21 have parley: like to talk

22 Stand fast: Hold your position; **out:** go out

24 Caesar: Octavius' full name was Octavius Caesar; **answer on their charge:** attack when they do

❓ Why do you think Antony calls Octavius by the name of Caesar here?

25 Mark forth: We will go forward

26 Stir not: Do not move

The meeting between the generals results in posturing and an exchange of insults.

✱ **BRUTUS.** Words before blows; is it so, countrymen?

OCTAVIUS. Not that we love words better, as you do.

BRUTUS. Good words are better than bad strokes, Octavius.

ANTONY. In your bad strokes, Brutus, you give good words. 30
    Witness the hole you made in Caesar's heart,
    Crying "Long live, hail, Caesar!"

CASSIUS.   Antony,
    The posture of your blows are yet unknown,
    But, for your words, they rob the Hybla bees,
    And leave them honeyless.

ANTONY.   Not stingless too. 35

BRUTUS. O yes, and soundless too,
    For you have stolen their buzzing, Antony,
    And very wisely threat before you sting.

ANTONY. Villains, you did not so when your vile daggers
    Hack'd one another in the sides of Caesar. 40
    You show'd your teeth like apes and fawn'd like hounds
    And bow'd like bondmen, kissing Caesar's feet,
    Whilst damnèd Casca, like a cur, behind
    Struck Caesar on the neck. O you flatterers!

CASSIUS. Flatterers?—Now, Brutus, thank yourself! 45
    This tongue had not offended so today
    If Cassius might have rul'd.

OCTAVIUS. Come, come, the cause. If arguing make us sweat,
    The proof of it will turn to redder drops.
    Look, I draw a sword against conspirators. 50

[He draws.]

---

33 posture of your blows: kind of blows you are able to produce

34 Hybla: a place in Sicily that is famous for its honey. This is a reference to Antony's sweet words to Cassius and Brutus after Caesar's death.

41 show'd your teeth: grinned

43 cur: dog

47 might have rul'd: had prevailed

❓ To what is Cassius referring in lines 45–47?

48 the cause: Let us focus on the business at hand.

49 The proof ... drops: Settling it in battle will turn our sweat into bloody drops.

PERSONA JOURNAL

Describe the scene as the generals trade insults and the two armies wait behind them.

✱ **"Sticks and Stones..."** The following exchange of insults may sound somewhat childish to today's readers and viewers—rather like the taunts of playground bullies. But in Shakespeare's time, it was customary for enemy generals to shout insults at each other before going into battle.

The insults continue and the meeting ends. Octavius and Antony return to their armies to make ready for the battle. Brutus and Cassius begin to give instructions to their men.

Act V   Scene i

When think you that the sword goes up again?
✳ Never, till Caesar's three and thirty wounds
  Be well aveng'd, or till another Caesar
  Have added slaughter to the sword of traitors.

BRUTUS. Caesar, thou canst not die by traitors' hands   55
  Unless thou bring'st them with thee.

OCTAVIUS.   So I hope.
  I was not born to die on Brutus' sword.

BRUTUS. O, if thou wert the noblest of thy strain,
  Young man, thou couldst not die more honourable.

CASSIUS. A peevish schoolboy, worthless of such honour,   60
  Join'd with a masker and a reveler!

ANTONY. Old Cassius still.

OCTAVIUS.   Come, Antony, away!
  Defiance, traitors, hurl we in your teeth.
  If you dare fight today, come to the field;
  If not, when you have stomachs.   65

[*Exit* OCTAVIUS, ANTONY, *and army.*]

CASSIUS. Why now, blow wind, swell billow, and swim bark!
  The storm is up, and all is on the hazard.

BRUTUS. Ho, Lucilius, hark, a word with you.

[LUCILIUS *and* MESSALA *stand forth.*]

LUCILIUS.   My lord?

51 goes up: will be put away

53–54 till another ... slaughter: until you kill Octavius Caesar and add another death

58 wert: were; **strain:** family

60 peevish: childish

61 masker and a reveler: refers to Antony, who has the reputation of being a party-goer

62 Old Cassius still: The same old Cassius

63 teeth: face

65 stomachs: courage

PERSONA ACTION

Personas with Antony return to camp.

66 blow wind ... bark: let the wind blow, the ocean swell, and our ship sail

67 on the hazard: at risk

✳ **Fact or Fiction?** Actually, Plutarch clearly stated that Caesar suffered from 23 wounds. So why does Shakespeare increase that number to 33? One critic has suggested the number has religious meaning; Jesus is traditionally believed to have been 33 years old when he was crucified.

164

Cassius worries about having to wager everything on just one battle. He has become more superstitious of late and tells Messala that the two eagles that have been like mascots to the troops have suddenly disappeared and been replaced by scavenger birds such as vultures and crows.

[BRUTUS *and* LUCILIUS *speak apart.*]

CASSIUS. Messala.

MESSALA.   What says my general?

CASSIUS.   Messala,
     This is my birthday, as this very day   70
     Was Cassius born. Give me thy hand, Messala.
     Be thou my witness that against my will,
     (As Pompey was) am I compell'd to set
     Upon one battle all our liberties.
✱   You know that I held Epicurus strong   75
     And his opinion. Now I change my mind
     And partly credit things that do presage.
     Coming from Sardis, on our former ensign
     Two mighty eagles fell, and there they perch'd,
     Gorging and feeding from our soldiers' hands,   80
     Who to Philippi here consorted us.
     This morning are they fled away and gone,
     And in their steads do ravens, crows, and kites
     Fly o'er our heads and downward look on us
     As we were sickly prey. Their shadows seem   85
     A canopy most fatal, under which
     Our army lies, ready to give up the ghost.

MESSALA. Believe not so.

CASSIUS.   I but believe it partly,
     For I am fresh of spirit and resolv'd
     To meet all perils very constantly.   90

BRUTUS. Even so, Lucilius.

---

70 as: on

73 As Pompey: Pompey was convinced to fight Caesar at Pharsalia against his better judgement.

75 held Epicurus strong: believed in the teachings of Epicurus. The Epicurean philosophy did not believe in omens or signs foretelling good or bad luck.

77 presage: predict the future

78 former ensign: foremost standard or banner

PERSONA JOURNAL

Do you believe in omens? Why or why not?

81 Who to ... us: Those same eagles accompanied us here to Philippi.

83 steads: place

85 As: As if; **sickly prey:** about to die

❓ Why is Cassius doubtful about the outcome of the battle?

87 give up the ghost: to die

90 very constantly: with determination

✱ **Epicureanism** The Greek philosopher Epicurus (341–270 B.C.) believed that pleasure was the highest good and led to a truly moral life. By pleasure, Epicurus meant living simply and moderately, not excessively or indulgently. He was also opposed to superstition of any kind. Many important people in history have called themselves epicureans—including Thomas Jefferson. But the word has come to be misused. Today, we think of an epicurean as one who selfishly indulges in sensual pleasures—especially fine food and wine.

Cassius and Brutus acknowledge that if the battle goes badly for them that this will be the last time they will speak. Brutus says that while he finds suicide cowardly, he would never allow himself to be taken prisoner.

[BRUTUS *returns to* CASSIUS.]

CASSIUS.   Now, most noble Brutus,
   The gods today stand friendly that we may,
   Lovers in peace, lead on our days to age.
   But since the affairs of men rests still incertain,
   Let's reason with the worst that may befall.   95
   If we do lose this battle, then is this
   The very last time we shall speak together.
   What are you then determinèd to do?

BRUTUS. Even by the rule of that philosophy
   By which I did blame Cato for the death   100
   Which he did give himself (I know not how,
   But I do find it cowardly and vile,
   For fear of what might fall, so to prevent
   The time of life) arming myself with patience
   To stay the providence of some high powers   105
   That govern us below.

CASSIUS.   Then, if we lose this battle,
   You are contented to be led in triumph
   Through the streets of Rome?

BRUTUS. No, Cassius, no. Think not, thou noble Roman,
   That ever Brutus will go bound to Rome.   110
   He bears too great a mind. But this same day
   Must end that work the ides of March begun.
   And whether we shall meet again, I know not.
   Therefore our everlasting farewell take.
   Forever and forever farewell, Cassius.   115
   If we do meet again, why we shall smile;
   If not, why then this parting was well made.

92 The gods: May the gods

93 Lovers: Friends; **lead on ... age:** grow old

94 rests still incertain: always remain uncertain

95 Let's reason ... befall: Let's assume that the worst might happen.

96 is this: this is

99 that: Stoic. The Stoic philosophy deemed suicide a cowardly act.

100 Cato: Marcus Cato, Portia's father, killed himself rather than surrender to Julius Caesar after Pompey's defeat at Pharsalia.

103 fall: happen

103–104 so to ... life: to end one's life before the natural life span

105 To stay ... powers: To await the will of the gods

106–107 led in ... Rome: paraded through the streets of Rome as a captive

PERSONA JOURNAL

Describe a victory parade with captives that you have seen in Rome.

PERSONA ACTION

Personas with Brutus return to camp.

CASSIUS. Forever and forever farewell, Brutus.
✱ If we do meet again, we'll smile indeed;
   If not, 'tis true this parting was well made.   120

BRUTUS. Why then, lead on.—O, that a man might know
   The end of this day's business ere it come!
   But it sufficeth that the day will end,
   And then the end is known.—Come ho, away!

[Exeunt.]

Richard Chamberlain as
Octavius in the 1970 film
directed by Stuart Burge.

✱ **"If we do meet again, we'll smile indeed."** When the British actor Ian Richardson played Cassius in a production of *Julius Caesar*, this was the key moment in his performance. Throughout the rest of the play, Richardson played Cassius as "stony-faced" and unsmiling. But at this tender moment of farewell to Brutus, he smiled at last. The audience was deeply moved.

TALES FROM THE STAGE
The Booth Brothers

The three actor brothers—Junius Brutus Booth Jr., Edwin Booth, and John Wilkes Booth—were considered the finest American Shakespearean players of their time. They were the sons of Junius Brutus Booth (1796–1852), an English actor who achieved great success in his native country before moving to America in 1821.

Julius Caesar was a favorite play of all three younger Booths. In 1864 the brothers created a sensation in New York by appearing together in *Julius Caesar*. It was a benefit performance to raise money for a statue of William Shakespeare—a statue still standing today in New York's Central Park. Edwin played Brutus, Junius played Cassius, and John Wilkes played Antony.

The Civil War was raging during this famous performance. Both Edwin and Junius Booth were solid supporters of the Union; only John Wilkes was a Southern sympathizer. Despite his great success in many Shakespearean roles, John Wilkes never achieved the same acclaim as his father or his brothers—especially Edwin, who was widely regarded as the greatest actor of his age.

On the afternoon of April 14, 1865—only a few months after that legendary New York performance of *Julius Caesar*—John Wilkes Booth sat in a saloon in Washington, D.C., having a drink with a friend who teased him for not being as great an actor as his father. Booth replied that he would soon "be the most talked-about man in America."

He was telling the truth. That very night at Ford's Theatre in Washington, John Wilkes Booth assassinated President Abraham Lincoln, who was watching a comedy called *My American Cousin*.

Pictured below are the three Booth brothers in *Julius Caesar*. From the left, John Wilkes played Mark Antony, Edwin played Brutus, and Junius played Cassius.

Setting the Scene

JULIUS CAESAR

Act V, Scenes ii and iii *or* The Battle Begins

Critical Query: Who do you want to win this battle? Why?

Warm-Up Improv

In the past few days you have become more and more upset with your friends. They seem to be talking about you behind your back—whispering and giggling until you get close and then becoming silent. Finally, you angrily confront them until they confess: they've been planning a surprise birthday party for you!

From the Prop Box

- Papers
- Standard (banner) for Cassius
- Swords and daggers
- Victory wreath

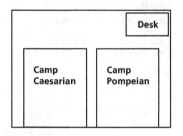

Classroom Set Design

The battlefield and two army camps as in the previous scene.

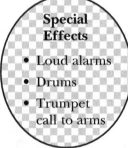

Special Effects

- Loud alarms
- Drums
- Trumpet call to arms

Word Play: Personification

Personification means attributing human characteristics to nonhuman things or concepts. For example, on page 175, lines 67–71, Messala likens "error" to a child that kills its mother, "melancholy."

Behind the Scene: Battle Plans

It is curious that Cassius continually let Brutus have his way, since Brutus' decisions often proved so disastrous. The Battle of Phillipi was no exception. Brutus and Cassius had an enviable position high up in the hills. They only had to wait for the arrival of Octavius and Antony who would have been completely vulnerable on the plains below. Instead, Brutus insisted on leaving the hills and going to meet the triumvirate. Even after losing this advantage, they might have taken the day. Brutus' forces easily won the first skirmish. Unfortunately, having experienced success, he allowed his men to relax and begin looting. Thus, when they were needed by Cassius on the other side of the battlefield they were unavailable. This error in judgment cost Cassius the victory and ultimately led to his despair and suicide.

Brutus, believing that Octavius' forces lack spirit, gives Messala written instructions ordering the troops on the other side of the field to attack immediately.

✻ Scene ii. Near Philippi. The Field of Battle

[Alarum. Enter BRUTUS *and* MESSALA.*]*

BRUTUS. Ride, ride, Messala, ride, and give these bills
   Unto the legions on the other side!

[He hands MESSALA *the papers.]*

[Loud alarum.]

   Let them set on at once, for I perceive
   But cold demeanour in Octavius' wing,
   And sudden push gives them the overthrow.   5
   Ride, ride, Messala! Let them all come down.

[Exeunt.]

Alarum: trumpets or drums calling the army to battle

1 bills: orders

2 other side: meaning the soldiers on the other side of the battlefield commanded by Cassius

4 But cold demeanour: A lack of fighting spirit

5 sudden push ... overthrow: a sudden attack will defeat them

6 them all: the entire army

❓ Why is Brutus so anxious to get the message to Cassius quickly?

Brutus. Detail from a drawing by J. Koghlan, ©1800.

✻ **The Scenic Route** For a couple of centuries, Shakespeare's plays were presented with huge sets and lumbering scene changes which bogged down the action. Shakespeare's original staging at the Globe was much more fast and fluid, with location changes often suggested simply by offstage noises and the entrances and exits of actors. Consider this exciting scene, which is only six lines long; it flowed without interruption between Scenes i and iii.

Cassius expresses his anger to Titinius because his own troops are fleeing. Titinius blames their circumstances on Brutus for attacking too early and leaving them vulnerable. Pindarus enters and urges Cassius to retreat. Cassius decides to send Titinius to a group of troops in the distance to discover if they are friend or foe.

Scene iii. Another Part of the Field

[Alarums. Enter CASSIUS, *carrying a standard, and* TITINIUS.*]*

CASSIUS. O look, Titinius, look, the villains fly!
    Myself have to mine own turn'd enemy.
    This ensign here of mine was turning back;
    I slew the coward and did take it from him.

TITINIUS. O Cassius, Brutus gave the word too early,   5
    Who, having some advantage on Octavius,
    Took it too eagerly. His soldiers fell to spoil,
    Whilst we by Antony are all enclosed.

[Enter PINDARUS.*]*

PINDARUS. Fly further off, my lord, fly further off!
    Mark Antony is in your tents, my lord.   10
    Fly therefore, noble Cassius, fly far off.

CASSIUS. This hill is far enough.—Look, look, Titinius,
    Are those my tents where I perceive the fire?

TITINIUS. They are, my lord.

CASSIUS.   Titinius, if thou lovest me,
    Mount thou my horse and hide thy spurs in him   15
    Till he have brought thee up to yonder troops
    And here again, that I may rest assur'd
    Whether yond troops are friend or enemy.

TITINIUS. I will be here again even with a thought.

[Exit TITINIUS.*]*

1 the villains fly: my own cowardly troops are running away!

2 Myself have ... enemy: I have become the enemy of my own soldiers.

3 ensign: standard bearer

4 it: the standard

5 the word: orders to attack

7 spoil: looting

❓ Who is to blame for Cassius' men being surrounded by Antony's troops?

8 all enclosed: surrounded

19 with a thought: with the speed of a thought

Cassius tells Pindarus to go to the top of the hill and report back to him about what he sees on the battlefield. Pindarus reports that Titinius has been surrounded and captured.

✻ CASSIUS. Go, Pindarus, get higher on that hill.   20
     My sight was ever thick. Regard Titinius
     And tell me what thou not'st about the field.

[*Exit* PINDARUS.]

     This day I breathèd first. Time is come round,
     And where I did begin, there shall I end;
     My life is run his compass.—Sirrah, what news?   25

PINDARUS. [*Above*] O my lord!

CASSIUS. What news?

PINDARUS. Titinius is enclosèd round about
     With horsemen that make to him on the spur,
     Yet he spurs on. Now they are almost on him.   30
     Now Titinius! Now some light. O, he lights too!

21 ever thick: always bad

22 not'st: observe

23 This day … first: On this day I took my first breath.

25 is run his compass: has completed its full circle

29 make to … spur: approach him at full speed

31 light: dismount

The battle at Phillipi. Mankiewicz film, 1953.

✻ **High Times** Cassius orders Pindarus to "get higher on that hill" for a better view of the battle. But where did Pindarus go in Shakespeare's original production? Did he go to the gallery above the stage, despite the fact that it was often used for audience seating? Did he go to a window near the gallery? Or did he simply go upstage—that is, farther back on the stage? Look at the diagram of the Globe Theatre on page 199 and make your own guess.

He's ta'en.

[Shout]

        And hark, they shout for joy.

CASSIUS. Come down, behold no more.—
    O, coward that I am to live so long
    To see my best friend ta'en before my face.   35

[PINDARUS comes down.]

    Come hither, sirrah.
    In Parthia did I take thee prisoner,
    And then I swore thee, saving of thy life,
    That whatsoever I did bid thee do
    Thou shouldst attempt it. Come now, keep thine oath.   40
    Now be a freeman, and with this good sword,
    That ran through Caesar's bowels, search this bosom.
    Stand not to answer. Here, take thou the hilts,
    And, when my face is cover'd, as 'tis now,
    Guide thou the sword.

[PINDARUS stabs him.]

              Caesar, thou art reveng'd,   45
    Even with the sword that kill'd thee.

[Dies.]

PINDARUS. So I am free, yet would not so have been,
    Durst I have done my will.—O Cassius!—
    Far from this country Pindarus shall run,
    Where never Roman shall take note of him.   50

[Exit PINDARUS.]

37 **Parthia:** an ancient country in what is now northern Iran

38 **swore thee:** made you swear

42 **search this bosom:** pierce my chest

43 **Stand not to answer:** Do not hesitate; **hilts:** handle of the sword

❓ In your opinion, why doesn't Cassius wait until the end of the battle to take his own life?

Titinius and Messala arrive with good news from the battle. Brutus has been victorious over Octavius. What Pindarus thought were enemy soldiers surrounding Titinius were actually Brutus' troops celebrating. Messala and Titinius find Cassius' body.

[Enter TITINIUS *and* MESSALA.*]*

MESSALA. It is but change, Titinius, for Octavius
    Is overthrown by noble Brutus' power,
    As Cassius' legions are by Antony.

51 change: an even exchange

TITINIUS. These tidings will well comfort Cassius.

MESSALA. Where did you leave him?

TITINIUS.   All disconsolate,   55
    With Pindarus his bondman, on this hill.

55 All disconsolate: Very dejected

MESSALA. Is not that he that lies upon the ground?

TITINIUS. He lies not like the living. O my heart!

Titinius (Jack Stehlihn) and Cassius (Edward Herrmann).
New York Shakespeare Festival, 1988.

© George E. Joseph

Titinius and Messala mourn Cassius. Titinius says that he will go to look for Pindarus while Messala leaves to tell Brutus the news of Cassius' death.

MESSALA. Is not that he?

TITINIUS.   No, this was he, Messala,
But Cassius is no more. O setting sun,   60
As in thy red rays thou dost sink to night,
So in his red blood Cassius' day is set.
The sun of Rome is set. Our day is gone;
Clouds, dews, and dangers come. Our deeds are done.
Mistrust of my success hath done this deed.   65

MESSALA. Mistrust of good success hath done this deed.
O hateful error, melancholy's child,
Why dost thou show to the apt thoughts of men
The things that are not? O error, soon conceiv'd,
Thou never com'st unto a happy birth   70
But kill'st the mother that engendr'd thee.

TITINIUS. What, Pindarus! Where are thou, Pindarus?

MESSALA. Seek him, Titinius, whilst I go to meet
The noble Brutus, thrusting this report
Into his ears. I may say "thrusting it,"   75
For piercing steel and darts envenomèd
Shall be as welcome to the ears of Brutus
As tidings of this sight.

TITINIUS.   Hie you, Messala,
And I will seek for Pindarus the while.

[Exit Messala.]

Why didst thou send me forth, brave Cassius?   80
Did I not meet thy friends, and did not they
Put on my brows this wreath of victory,

65 my success: the results of my mission

66 good success: the general outcome of the battle

68 apt: receptive

71 mother that ... thee: the melancholy person that gave you life

76 darts envenomèd: poisoned arrows

78 Hie you: Go quickly

❓ What was the confusion that caused Cassius to commit suicide?

Titinius is overcome with grief. He crowns the slain Cassius with a victory wreath and then commits suicide using the same sword that killed Cassius. Brutus and his staff arrive to discover both Cassius and Titinius dead.

> And bid me give it thee? Didst thou not hear their shouts?
> Alas, thou hast misconstru'd everything.
> But hold thee, take this garland on thy brow.   85

[Laying the garland on CASSIUS' *brow.]*

> Thy Brutus bid me give it thee, and I
> Will do his bidding.—Brutus, come apace,
> And see how I regarded Caius Cassius.—
> By your leave, gods, this is a Roman's part.
> Come, Cassius' sword, and find Titinius' heart!   90

[He dies on CASSIUS' *sword.]*

[Alarum. Enter BRUTUS, MESSALA, YOUNG CATO, STRATO, VOLUMNIUS, *and* LUCILIUS, LABEO, *and* FLAVIUS.*]*

BRUTUS. Where, where, Messala, doth his body lie?

MESSALA. Lo, yonder, and Titinius mourning it.

BRUTUS. Titinius' face is upward.

CATO.   He is slain.

✱ **BRUTUS.** O Julius Caesar, thou art mighty yet;
> Thy spirit walks abroad and turns our swords   95
> In our own proper entrails.

[Low alarums.]

CATO.   Brave Titinius!
> Look whe'r he have not crowned dead Cassius.

BRUTUS. Are yet two Romans living such as these?
> The last of all the Romans, fare thee well.
> It is impossible that ever Rome   100

84 misconstru'd: misinterpreted

87 apace: quickly

89 By your leave: With your permission; **part:** duty

❓ Why do you think Titinius takes his life?

96 own proper entrails: very own guts

❓ Why does Brutus say that Caesar still has power?

✱ **"O Julius Caesar, thou art mighty yet ..."** The spirit of Caesar was mighty, indeed, among the English of Shakespeare's time. They knew the general had made some raids into Britain, and they made up legends about his contributions to their culture. For example, they credited him with starting to build the Tower of London—a story that Shakespeare repeats in *Richard III*. Actually, the Tower's construction was begun by William the Conqueror after his invasion of England in 1066.

Should breed thy fellow.—Friends, I owe more tears
To this dead man than you shall see me pay.—
I shall find time, Cassius; I shall find time.—
Come, therefore, and to Thasos send his body.
His funerals shall not be in our camp,   105
Lest it discomfort us.—Lucilius, come.—
And come, young Cato. Let us to the field.—
Labeo and Flavius, set our battles on.
'Tis three o'clock, and, Romans, yet ere night
We shall try fortune in a second fight.   110

[Exeunt.]

101 thy fellow: your equal

104 Thasos: an island near Philippi where Plutarch says Cassius was buried

106 discomfort us: depress our troops

108 battles on: armies forward

Setting the Scene
JULIUS CAESAR
Act V, Scenes iv and v *or* The Battle's Over

Critical Query: How do you think the future will unfold?

Classroom Set Design

There are still two army camps but the playing area will represent a different part of the battlefield in each scene. In Scene v there is a large rock (use chairs or student desks) that Brutus and Clitis sit on.

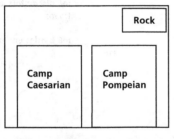

Literary Lore: Theme

A theme is an ongoing topic, idea, or concern of a literary work. Of course, one theme of *Julius Caesar* is the nature of power—how it is gained and lost, how it is used and misused. But a play this complex will contain many other themes. What others can you name?

Famous Quotes from Scene v

- This was the noblest Roman of them all.
- His life was gentle and the elements so mix'd in him that nature might stand up and say to all the world "This was a man."

In Character: Ghostly Panel

Various students will sit in a group of three hot seats portraying the ghosts of Caesar, Cassius, and Brutus while the rest of the class questions them about events in the play and the final outcome.

Special Effects

- Alarms
- Drums
- Trumpet calls to arms and to retreat

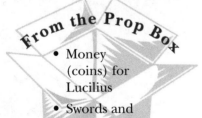

From the Prop Box

- Money (coins) for Lucilius
- Swords and daggers

Warm-Up Improv

You are a political candidate who's run an exhausting race. Now you wait with good friends for the votes to come in. At first it seems as though you have a chance, but it soon becomes evident that things will not go your way—you are going to lose. You give a brief farewell speech to your friends and campaign workers.

At the battlefront, Brutus encourages his troops to fight. When several of his men are overwhelmed by Antony's soldiers, one of them, Lucilius, valiantly tries to draw attention away from his leader by pretending to be Brutus.

Scene iv. Another Part of the Field

[Alarum. Enter BRUTUS, MESSALA, YOUNG CATO, LUCILIUS, *and* FLAVIUS.*]*

BRUTUS. Yet, countrymen, O, yet hold up your heads!

[Exit, with MESSALA *and* FLAVIUS.*]*

YOUNG CATO. What bastard doth not? Who will go with me?
    I will proclaim my name about the field.
    I am the son of Marcus Cato, ho!
    A foe to tyrants, and my country's friend.   5
✱ I am the son of Marcus Cato, ho!

[Enter Soldiers and fight.]

LUCILIUS. And I am Brutus, Marcus Brutus, I!
    Brutus, my country's friend! Know me for Brutus.

[Young CATO *is slain.]*

    O young and noble Cato, art thou down?
    Why, now thou diest as bravely as Titinius,   10
    And mayst be honored, being Cato's son.

FIRST SOLDIER. Yield, or thou diest.

LUCILIUS.   Only I yield to die.
    There is so much that thou wilt kill me straight:

[Offering money.]

    Kill Brutus and be honoured in his death.

[FIRST] SOLDIER. We must not. A noble prisoner!   15

[Enter ANTONY.*]*

2 bastard: person of low birth

3 about: around

12 Only I ... die: I will surrender only when you kill me.

13 straight: immediately

❓ Why does Lucilius offer the enemy soldier money?

✱ **"I am the son of Marcus Cato, ho!"** Young Cato is not only boasting of being the son of an illustrious Roman, but also of his close kinship to Brutus. Marcus Porcius Cato (95–46 B.C.) was Portia's father and Brutus' uncle.

Antony is called to witness the captured "Brutus." Antony recognizes Lucilius and sends his men on to search for the real Brutus.

Act V   Scene iv

SECOND SOLDIER. Room, ho! Tell Antony Brutus is ta'en.

FIRST SOLDIER. I'll tell the news. Here comes the General.—
   Brutus is ta'en, Brutus is ta'en, my lord.

ANTONY. Where is he?

LUCILIUS. Safe, Antony, Brutus is safe enough.   20
   I dare assure thee that no enemy
   Shall ever take alive the noble Brutus.
   The gods defend him from so great a shame.
   When you do find him, or alive or dead,
   He will be found like Brutus, like himself.   25

✱ **ANTONY.** This is not Brutus, friend; but, I assure you,
   A prize no less in worth. Keep this man safe;
   Give him all kindness. I had rather have
   Such men my friends than enemies. Go on,
   And see whe'er Brutus be alive or dead,   30
   And bring us word unto Octavius' tent
   How every thing is chanc'd.

   [Exeunt in different directions.]

16 Room: Make room

25 like himself: true to his noble nature

❓ Does Antony's reaction to Lucilius surprise you? Explain.

32 is chanc'd: has turned out

✱ **Compare and Contrast** Antony's speech about Lucilius' capture is very close to Plutarch's version. Consider how Shakespeare turned it into dramatic poetry. Plutarch: "My companions, I think you are sorry you have failed of your purpose, and that you think this man hath done you great wrong; but I do assure you, you have taken a better booty than that you followed. For instead of an enemy, you have brought me a friend ... For I had rather have such men my friends, as this man here, than enemies."

On another part of the battlefield, Brutus is accompanied by several of his men. Since it appears that the battle is lost, Brutus asks first Clitus and then Dardanius to help him die. Both men refuse.

Scene v. Another Part of the Field

[Enter BRUTUS, DARDANIUS, CLITUS, STRATO, and VOLUMNIUS.]

❋ **BRUTUS.** Come, poor remains of friends, rest on this rock.

[He sits down.]

CLITUS. Statilius showed the torchlight, but, my lord,
    He came not back. He is or ta'en or slain.

BRUTUS. Sit thee down, Clitus. Slaying is the word;
    It is a deed in fashion. Hark thee, Clitus.   5

[Whispers.]

CLITUS. What, I, my lord? No, not for all the world.

BRUTUS. Peace, then, no words.

CLITUS.   I'll rather kill myself.

BRUTUS. Hark thee, Dardanius.

[Whispers.]

DARDANIUS.   Shall I do such a deed?

CLITUS. O Dardanius!

DARDANIUS. O Clitus!   10

[DARDANIUS and CLITUS step aside.]

CLITUS. What ill request did Brutus make to thee?

DARDANIUS. To kill him, Clitus. Look, he meditates.

---

1 poor remains of: those of my friends that still remain alive

2 showed the torchlight: gave the signal by the light of his torch

3 or ta'en or slain: either captured or killed

5 deed in fashion: a common occurrence these days

❋ **Rocky Road** Elizabethan staging was simple, with a minimum of scenery. So was the rock that Brutus mentions actually brought onstage for this scene? Although such a rock is listed among stage props (properties) for one of Shakespeare's rival companies, it seems unlikely that a rock was dragged out for this scene. If Brutus and his companions simply sat on the stage itself, Shakespeare's audience was imaginative enough to visualize a rock.

Brutus calls Volumnius and tells him of the two appearances of Caesar's ghost. Brutus interprets this as indicating it is time for his death and asks Volumnius to hold his sword so that he might run onto it. Volumnius refuses. Clitus enters and urgently tells them all to flee. Brutus begins to say farewell to his men.

CLITUS. Now is that noble vessel full of grief,
　　That it runs over even at his eyes.

BRUTUS. Come hither, good Volumnius. List a word.　　　15

VOLUMNIUS. What says my lord?

BRUTUS.　　　　　　　　　Why this, Volumnius;
　　The ghost of Caesar hath appear'd to me
　　Two several times by night—at Sardis once
　　And this last night here in Philippi fields.
　　I know my hour is come.

VOLUMNIUS.　　　　　　Not so, my lord.　　　20

BRUTUS. Nay, I am sure it is, Volumnius.
　　Thou seest the world, Volumnius, how it goes.
　　Our enemies have beat us to the pit.

[Low alarums.]

　　It is more worthy to leap in ourselves
　　Than tarry till they push us. Good Volumnius,　　　25
　　Thou know'st that we two went to school together;
　　Even for that our love of old, I prithee,
　　Hold thou my sword hilts whilst I run on it.

VOLUMNIUS. That's not an office for a friend, my lord.

[Alarum continues.]

CLITUS. Fly, fly, my lord! There is no tarrying here.　　　30

BRUTUS. Farewell to you—and you—and you, Volumnius.—
　　Strato, thou hast been all this while asleep.
　　Farewell to thee too, Strato.—Countrymen,

15 List a word: Let me have a word with you.

18 several: separate

23 beat us to the pit: driven us to the edge of our graves

28 hilts: handle

29 an office: a task

30 There is … here: You can not linger here.

After the others leave, Brutus asks Strato to hold his sword. Strato does so; Brutus falls on the sword and dies.

My heart doth joy that yet in all my life
I found no man but he was true to me.   35
✱ I shall have glory by this losing day
More than Octavius and Mark Antony
By this vile conquest shall attain unto.
So fare you well at once, for Brutus' tongue
Hath almost ended his life's history.   40
Night hangs upon mine eyes; my bones would rest,
That have but laboured to attain this hour.

[Alarum. Cry within, "Fly, fly, fly!"]

CLITUS. Fly, my lord, fly!

BRUTUS.   Hence. I will follow.

[All exeunt but BRUTUS *and* STRATO.]

I prithee, Strato, stay thou by thy lord.
Thou art a fellow of a good respect;   45
Thy life hath had some smatch of honour in it.
Hold, then, my sword, and turn away thy face
While I do run upon it. Wilt thou, Strato?

STRATO. Give me your hand first. Fare you well, my lord.

BRUTUS. Farewell, good Strato.

[Runs on his sword.]

                         Caesar, now be still.   50
I kill'd not thee with half so good a will.

[Dies.]

[Alarum. Retreat. Enter ANTONY, OCTAVIUS, MESSALA, LUCILIUS, *and the army.]*

❓ What is ironic about lines 34–35?

39 at once: all together

PERSONA ACTION

From outside the playing area, personas convey the chaos of battle with cries of "flee."

45 respect: reputation
46 smatch: taste

51 I kill'd ... will: I did not kill you half so eagerly as I kill myself.

❓ Do you feel any differently about the death of Brutus than you did about the death of Cassius?

Retreat: a signal that announces the end of the battle

✱ **Is It Hot in Here?** *The Inferno* by Dante Alighieri (1265–1321) describes a journey into hell. Because Dante believed that there was no sin worse than betraying one's master, he put Cassius and Brutus in hell's very lowest level, along with Christ's betrayer, Judas. The three traitors are inside the mouth of Satan, who munches on their bodies throughout eternity. Do you think Shakespeare would have agreed with Dante's portrayal of Cassius' and Brutus' damnation?

The death of Brutus. Aquila Theatre Company, 2000.

Octavius, Antony, Messala, and Lucilius arrive to discover Strato with Brutus' body. They inquire as to how Brutus died and Strato tells them. Octavius offers to accept all those who served Brutus into his service. Antony eulogizes Brutus with glorious praise.

OCTAVIUS. What man is that?

MESSALA. My master's man.—Strato, where is thy master?

STRATO. Free from the bondage you are in, Messala.
The conquerors can but make a fire of him,   55
For Brutus only overcame himself,
And no man else hath honour by his death.

LUCILIUS. So Brutus should be found.—I thank thee, Brutus,
That thou hast prov'd Lucilius' saying true.

✱ OCTAVIUS. All that serv'd Brutus, I will entertain them.—   60
Fellow, wilt thou bestow thy time with me?

STRATO. Ay, if Messala will prefer me to you.

OCTAVIUS. Do so, good Messala.

MESSALA. How died my master, Strato?

STRATO. I held the sword, and he did run on it.   65

MESSALA. Octavius, then take him to follow thee,
That did the latest service to my master.

ANTONY. This was the noblest Roman of them all.
All the conspirators save only he
Did that they did in envy of great Caesar.   70
He only in a general honest thought
And common good to all made one of them.
His life was gentle and the elements
So mix'd in him that nature might stand up
And say to all the world "This was a man."   75

---

55 make a fire of: cremate

56 only overcame: alone conquered

59 Lucilius' saying true: refers to Act 5, Scene iv, lines 21–25

60 entertain them: take into my service

62 prefer: recommend

67 latest: ultimate

70 in envy of: out of jealousy and spite for

71–72 He only … them: Brutus was the only conspirator whose reasons for killing Caesar were honorable and for the common good of the Roman people.

73 gentle: noble; **elements:** elements of his character

✱ What's in a Name? When Octavius eventually became Rome's first emperor, he took the name Caesar Augustus, and "Caesar" became the title of Roman emperors who came after him. The titles of czar (for rulers of Russia) and Kaiser (for rulers of Germany) also came from the word Caesar.

Octavius, too, praises Brutus and calls for an end to the conflict.

Act V   Scene v

OCTAVIUS. According to his virtue, let us use him
  With all respect and rites of burial.
  Within my tent his bones tonight shall lie,
  Most like a soldier, order'd honourably.
  So call the field to rest, and let's away   80
  To part the glories of this happy day.

✳ *[Exeunt omnes.]*

76 use: treat

79 order'd honourably: treated with honor

80 field: army

81 part: share

❓ Are you surprised by Antony's and Octavius' response to Brutus' body?

PERSONA JOURNAL

How has this conflict affected you and your family?

LOYALTY CHECK

Make your final decision and explain your reasons in your journal.

Antony (Al Pacino) eulogizes the slain Brutus (Martin Sheen).
New York Shakespeare Festival, 1988.

© George E. Joseph

✳ **Happily Ever After** The Swiss traveler Thomas Platter kept a journal in which he described the original 1599 production of *Julius Caesar*. According to Platter, Shakespeare's players managed to end even this tragedy on a happy note. After the performance, he wrote, the actors "danced according to their custom with extreme elegance. Two in men's clothes and two in women's gave this performance, in wonderful combination with each other."

Reacting to Act V

Analysis

1. What is accomplished during the meeting in Scene i between the two sides? Why do you think this meeting took place?

2. In Scene i, what does Cassius tell Messala about his earlier philosophy? How has his viewpoint changed?

3. Why is suicide a difficult decision for Brutus?

4. At the time of his death, how does Brutus feel about his fortunes, as compared with those of the victors?

5. How sincere do you think Antony is when he praises Brutus at the end of the play? Explain your answer.

6. What are your final impressions of Brutus, Cassius, Octavius, and Antony?

Literary Elements

1. Good drama has **conflict**. Look at Scene i, when the four generals meet for their battle parley. Name some things that increase the tension in this scene.

2. **Personification** means attributing human characteristics to nonhuman things. Explain how "error" is personified in Scene iii.

3. **Mood**, or atmosphere, refers to the feelings the audience has toward the events of the play. For each of the scenes in Act V, try to pinpoint the mood and explain what language and imagery support your opinion.

4. **Dramatic irony** occurs when the audience knows something that the characters on stage do not. Explain the irony of Cassius' death.

Writing

1. Write a scene for the second appearance of Caesar's ghost as mentioned in Act 5, Scene v.

2. Write a news report from the battlefield describing the results of the fighting and the events of the day.

3. The Roman army was famous for its organization, discipline, and courage. Research some aspect of the Roman legions—their makeup, weapons, or tactics, for example—and write a report on what you find.

4. Brutus has been torn between his loyalties to his friend and leader—Caesar—and his loyalties to the Roman republic, and the values it stands for. To what people, beliefs, groups, or organizations do you feel strongly loyal? Write your response in a short essay. Include specific details, examples, and anecdotes that will help others understand your perspective. If you have trouble deciding your priorities, explain why you think that is.

Reacting to the Play

Analysis

1. How are the common people portrayed in *Julius Caesar*? Discuss what the play seems to say about democracy.

2. In Orson Welles' "modern dress" production of *Julius Caesar*, some actors wore black uniforms like those of European dictators in the 1930s. What parallels do you see between the plot of *Julius Caesar* and politics today?

3. Stoicism is a philosophy that promotes a detached, fatalistic view of one's own life. It holds that a person should endure with detachment and a tranquil heart both the pleasures and pains dealt out by fate. Trace how this Stoic philosophy affects Brutus' behavior and decisions throughout the play.

4. The conspirator Brutus believed that the immoral act of murder would in this case benefit all Romans. Do you agree that a noble end sometimes justifies less than noble means?

5. In your opinion, what do you think Shakespeare was saying about political power to his audience in the England of early 1600?

Literary Elements

1. In *Julius Caesar*, Shakespeare uses great insight to show the contrast between how **characters** see themselves and how they really are. Describe these different versions using a two-column chart. Do you notice a similar contrast in people you know?

2. As you might expect, this play about political beliefs and war is full of **conflict**. Name some ways in which Shakespeare increases the conflict via character personalities, relationships, language, and other plot devices.

3. Trace a strand of **imagery** that is repeated throughout the play, such as storms, blood, fire, or honor. Indicate where the image occurs and explain how it contributes to the meaning of the play.

4. In *Julius Caesar*, Shakespeare often used **imagery** related to the sky. Find such examples and discuss what the drama gains by these references.

5. Where do you believe the **climax**, or emotional highpoint, is in this play? Explain what you think Shakespeare may have intended by placing the climax here.

6. Review the definition of the **tragic hero** on page 23. How does Caesar and/or Brutus fit this definition? What are their tragic flaws?

Writing

1. Invent a new conclusion to the play *Julius Caesar* that shows what might have happened if Caesar had survived the attack at the Forum. Go back into the play as far as necessary to create a different ending. Write your new ending in play form.

2. Write a short parody of *Julius Caesar*.

3. Write an essay about one of the major themes found in *Julius Caesar*, which include ambition, greed, love, honesty, jealousy, and honor. Look for concrete examples of these qualities in the characters, events, and language of the play.

4. Caesar resisted warnings of the plots against him. As Caesar's chief of security, prepare a briefing that advises him of the people who are most dangerous to him and of your plans to protect him.

5. Write a scene between Portia and Calpurnia that takes place the first time they see each other after Caesar's death.

6. Although Caesar dies in Act III, Shakespeare titled his play *Julius Caesar*. Read the following statements and pick the one you most strongly agree with. Defend your choice with examples from the text.

a. Shakespeare's title is appropriate. Julius Caesar is the main character in this drama even though he dies in Act III.

b. The title *Julius Caesar* is weak. A better title could be found for this play. (Suggest one, and give reasons for your choice.)

Life in Ancient Rome

"Liberty! Freedom! Tyranny is dead!"

So cries Senator Cinna after Caesar's death in Shakespeare's *Julius Caesar*. Cinna wants all Romans to know that the assassination was not a simple act of brutality. It was committed to save the republic of Rome from a tyrant's rule.

Rome had become a republic back in 509 B.C.—more than four and a half centuries before the action of *Julius Caesar*. In theory, a republic is a form of government in which laws are made by democratically elected representatives. When the founders of our own nation framed the United States Constitution, they were partly inspired by the Roman republic.

Julius Caesar (100–44 B.C.), Roman statesman and general

But just how free and democratic was this republic?

In the time of Shakespeare's play, the main governing body of Rome was its Senate. This was a group of males of noble birth known as patricians. (Julius Caesar set the number of senators at 900.) Not really an elected body, the Senate was more like an exclusive club. One got to be a Senator through money and influence. The Senate was also extremely corrupt, with little concern for the welfare of the people.

Fortunately, the common people (the plebeians) also had governmental representatives called tribunes. The tribunes had the power to veto acts of the Senate and Rome's two most powerful leaders, the Consuls. The tribunes truly acted in the plebeians' best interests.

But despite the tribunes' efforts, life in Rome was unfair and unequal. Imagine yourself a traveler in the first century B.C., entering through a gate of the magnificent wall surrounding Rome. You would have been shocked by what you saw once you were inside.

Most of ancient Rome lacked the splendor portrayed in Hollywood movies. It was not filled with beautiful marble temples and palaces. Instead, about 90 percent of its total population (between 500,000 and 1 million people) lived in desperate poverty. Small shopkeepers lived in tiny rooms atop or behind their stalls. Still poorer people dressed in rags and lived in huts and shanties. Their dwellings were made of wood, so the city was constantly in danger of fires.

The wealthy ten percent of Romans—mostly patricians—lived in beautiful homes placed out of sight of all this poverty. Their houses had huge patios, fine murals, and sometimes private baths.

Patricians put on magnificent banquets, at which guests reclined on couches around a low dinner table. They ate with their hands, although sometimes they also used knives. Banquets included such exotic dishes as ostrich or flamingo. The fine wine was so strong that it usually had to be diluted with water. While banquet guests ate and drank, they were entertained by music, recitals of poetry, and cultivated conversation.

Not surprisingly, the patricians constantly worried that the plebeians would rise up in rebellion. So they carried out a policy called "bread and circuses." This meant offering the plebeians free food and diverting them with plays, gladiator fights, chariot races, and other forms of entertainment. The patricians also built magnificent bath houses, open to the public. These baths were rather like today's swimming pools, heated by hot coals underneath the floors.

The inequality of ancient Rome extended to its women. Even patrician women were considered of inferior status. Consider the following true story about Brutus' wife, Portia:

Before she married Brutus, Portia was the wife of a Roman patrician named Bibulus, with whom she had several sons. Another patrician named Quintus Hortensius approached Portia's father, Cato, with a proposition. He wanted to borrow Portia from Bibulus to be his own wife for a while, so she could produce heirs for him. Once Portia gave birth to a son or two for Quintus, Bibulus could have her back.

Cato respectfully refused Quintus' request. Even so, this sort of "wife swapping" was common in Rome—and women had no say in the matter. They were considered little more than the property of their husbands. Their duty was to manage patrician households, which were practically prisons to them.

Nevertheless, some Roman women (including Portia) achieved considerable prestige. They were educated along with boys until they were 12 years old, and some patrician women were allowed to continue their education on into adulthood. Though confined to their homes, Roman women sometimes distinguished themselves as poets, musicians, and visual artists.

They also had some surprising legal rights. For example, they were free to divorce their husbands. To legally do so, all a woman had to do was leave her husband's house for good, taking her dowry with her. According to Roman law, her husband could do nothing to get her  back. So even though a patrician husband regarded his wife as an item of property, he felt obliged to make her life reasonably pleasant.

Slavery was also an important part of Roman life. Whether or not one was a slave had nothing to do with race or ethnicity; it was typically a matter of being born into the slave class. As one might expect, most slaves endured hopeless lives of physical drudgery.

But there were quite a few interesting exceptions. Some slaves were highly educated and worked as actors, architects, singers, musicians, and teachers. Moreover, many slaves were freed by their masters. For example, if a physician trained a slave in medicine, he might free that slave to continue his practice after he died.

Other masters freed their slaves for business reasons. Some slaves worked as stewards—that is, as managers of patrician estates. A master might free a particularly intelligent and savvy steward and make him his business partner.

A freed slave (or freedman) was not a full-fledged Roman citizen, but his children were. In fact, the son of a freedman might become extremely wealthy and influential. Many Roman senators and patricians were the grandchildren of freed slaves.

So slavery wasn't necessarily an everlasting curse. A freedman's son generally had a better chance in life than a poor plebeian, who had no chance at all. Some patricians who lost their fortunes sold *themselves* into slavery as stewards, hoping for

better lives for their children and grandchildren.

Some patricians sold members of their own families into slavery for more sinister reasons. A patrician might sell his son just to punish him for disobedience, and to officially disinherit him. If this seems shocking, other aspects of Roman family life were more shocking still.

For example, the very moment a baby was born, the boy or girl was placed on the floor. If the father picked the baby up, he acknowledged the child as his son or daughter. But if the father left the baby on the floor, the boy or girl was taken away and "exposed"—abandoned in some public place. If the child was lucky, he or she would be adopted, probably as a slave. But most exposed children died.

This practice wasn't the least bit frowned upon. And it was as common among rich patricians as among poor plebeians. A wealthy man might simply decide that he had enough children and that the newborn infant should be gotten rid of. It doesn't seem to have much mattered whether the infant was a boy or a girl. Unsurprisingly, this was one of many decisions in which mothers had no say.

Whatever opinions we might have of life in the Roman republic, Shakespeare's Cinna spoke much too soon when he exclaimed, "Tyranny is dead!"

In 27 B.C., after the deaths of Brutus, Cassius, and Mark Antony, Octavius seized near-absolute power over even senators and tribunes. He became Rome's first emperor. Octavius adopted the name Caesar Augustus in honor of his uncle (and adoptive father) Julius Caesar. After his death, he was succeeded by other equally powerful emperors, all of whom went by the title of "Caesar."

So the Roman republic revered by Brutus came to an end. The Roman Empire had begun, and would dominate the western world for another five centuries.

Actor playing Marcus Junius Brutus (85–42 B.C.), Roman statesman

Shakespeare's Life

Many great authors can be imagined as living among the characters in their works. Historical records reveal how these writers spoke, felt, and thought. But Shakespeare is more mysterious. He never gave an interview or wrote an autobiography—not even one of his letters survives. What we know about his life can be told very briefly.

Shakespeare was born in April 1564. The exact date of his birth is unknown, but he was baptized on April 26 in the Stratford-upon-Avon church. His father, John, was a prominent local man who served as town chamberlain and mayor. Young William attended grammar school in Stratford, where he would have learned Latin—a requirement for a professional career—and some Greek.

Shakespeare's schoolroom

In 1582, William married Anne Hathaway. He was eighteen; she was twenty-six. At the time of their marriage, Anne was already three months pregnant with their first daughter, Susanna. In 1585, the couple had twins, Judith and Hamnet. Hamnet died before reaching adulthood, leaving Shakespeare no male heir.

Even less than usual is known about Shakespeare's life between 1585 and 1592. During that time, he moved to London and became an actor and playwright. He left his family behind in Stratford. Although he surely visited them occasionally, we have little evidence about what Shakespeare was like as a father and a husband.

Several of his early plays were written during this time, including *The Comedy of Errors, Titus Andronicus,* and the three parts of *Henry VI.* In those days, working in the theatre was rather like acting in soap operas today—the results may be popular, but daytime serials aren't recognized as serious art. In fact, many people were opposed to even allowing plays to be performed. Ministers warned their congregations of the dangers of going to plays.

But Shakespeare and his friends were lucky. Queen Elizabeth I loved plays. She protected acting companies from restrictive laws and gave them her permission to perform.

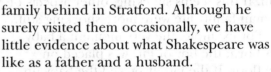

Queen Elizabeth I

Shakespeare wrote several plays to be performed for the queen, including *Twelfth Night*.

After Elizabeth's death in 1603, Shakespeare's company became known as the King's Men. This group of actors performed for James I, who had ruled Scotland before becoming king of England. Perhaps to thank James for his patronage, Shakespeare wrote *Macbeth*, which included two topics of strong interest to the king—Scottish royalty and witchcraft.

Unlike many theatre people, Shakespeare actually earned a good living. By 1599, he was part-owner of the Globe, one of the newest theatres in London. Such plays as *Othello, Hamlet,* and *King Lear* were first performed there.

In 1610 or 1611, Shakespeare moved back to the familiar surroundings of Stratford-upon-Avon. He was almost fifty years old, well past middle age by 17th-century standards. Over the years, he'd invested in property around Stratford, acquiring a comfortable estate and a family coat of arms.

But Shakespeare didn't give up writing. In 1611, his new play *The Tempest* was performed at Court. In 1613, his play *Henry VIII* premiered. This performance was more dramatic than anyone had expected. The stage directions called for a cannon to be fired when "King Henry" came on stage. The explosion set the stage on fire, and the entire theatre burned to the ground.

Shakespeare died in 1616 at the age of fifty-two. Scholars have wondered why he willed his "second-best bed" to his widow, but he also left Anne his plays and a comfortable income. His gravestone carried this inscription:

> Good friend for Jesus sake forbear
> To dig the dust enclosed here!
> Blest be the man that spares these stones,
> And curst be he that moves my bones.

Shakespeare's Times:
The Question of Succession

Why did William Shakespeare decide to set a tragedy in ancient Rome? Paradoxically, Shakespeare may have written about the past because of what was happening in his present. Queen Elizabeth I had come to power because the king had no male heir. She was popular, but also old and childless. Her subjects were concerned about who would succeed her. Some were even ready to depose her (just as some Romans had been ready to overthrow Julius Caesar).

Plots to overthrow the queen defied the common belief that God appointed sovereigns. According to the doctrine of divine right, subjects had no right to change rulers. Among her enemies was the charismatic Earl of Essex, who believed that it was time for a strong, young king—like himself—to take the throne. Essex was eventually beheaded for treason.

The story of Julius Caesar also had striking parallels to the politics of Shakespeare's time. Like Brutus and Caesar, Essex and Elizabeth had once been close friends. Like Brutus, Essex invoked honor and patriotism to support his arguments.

Like Brutus, Essex was willing to shed blood to achieve his goals. Finally, the question of succession was a burning issue in both eras.

Of course, there were also significant differences between England and Rome. For one, the Romans had to choose between two forms of government: a republic or an absolute ruler. The English simply had to identify a new monarch. These differences allowed Shakespeare to write about contemporary politics without personal risk.

Julius Caesar was first performed in 1599, the midpoint of Shakespeare's career. The play can be thought of as either a history or tragedy. Like most tragedies, it describes the pride and fall of powerful people. Like most histories, it has no clear-cut villain, so it is open to interpretation. During some periods, the murder of Caesar has been seen as justified; during others, it has been considered treason.

With this history-tragedy, Shakespeare began moving into his great tragic themes. In his book *Shakespeare*, Anthony Burgess says that the playwright became preoccupied with "the puzzle of the good intention that could produce evil . . . . Brutus was a murderer, but still the noblest Roman of them all. The conscience of the killer was to become an obsessive theme in the tragedies Shakespeare was preparing to write."

Why was Shakespeare suddenly fascinated with evil? We may never know, for Shakespeare's life remains a mystery.

Shakespeare's Theatre

In Shakespeare's London, a day's entertainment often began with a favorite amusement, bearbaiting. A bear would be captured and chained to a stake inside a pit. A pack of dogs would be released, and they would attack the bear. Spectators placed bets on which would die first. Admission to these pits cost only a penny, so they were very popular with working-class Londoners.

After the bearbaiting was over, another penny purchased admission to a play. Each theatre had its own company of actors, often supported by a nobleman or a member of the royal family.

As part-owner of the Globe Theatre, Shakespeare wrote plays, hired actors, and paid the bills. Since the Globe presented a new play every three weeks, Shakespeare and his actors had little time to rehearse or polish their productions. To complicate matters even more, most actors played more than one part in a play.

Boys played all the female roles. Most acting companies had three or four youths who were practically raised in the theatre. They started acting as early as age seven and

The Swan Theatre in London, drawn by Arend van Buchell in 1596

played female roles until they began shaving. Actresses would not become part of the English theatre for another fifty years.

The audience crowded into the theatre at about 2 p.m. The cheapest seats weren't seats at all but standing room in front of the stage. This area, known as the "pit," was occupied by "groundlings" or "penny knaves," who could be more trouble to the actors than they were worth. If the play was boring, the groundlings would throw rotten eggs or vegetables. They talked loudly to their friends, played cards, and even picked fights with each other. One theatre was set on fire by audience members who didn't like the play.

The theatre was open to the sky, so rain or snow presented a problem. However, the actors were partially protected by a roof known as the "heavens," and wealthier patrons sat in three stories of sheltered galleries that surrounded the pit and most of the main stage.

The main stage, about twenty-five-feet deep and forty-five-feet wide, projected into the audience, so spectators were closely involved in the action. This stage was rather bare, with only a few pieces of furniture. But this simplicity allowed for flexible and fluid staging. Unlike too many later productions, plays at the Globe did not grind to a halt for scene changes. When one group of actors exited through a doorway and a new group entered through another, Shakespeare's audience understood that a new location was probably being represented.

So the action of the plays was exciting and swift. The Chorus of *Romeo and Juliet* speaks of "the two hours' traffic of our stage," which suggests a rate of performance and delivery that today's actors would find nearly impossible.

Behind the main stage was the "tiring-house" where the actors changed costumes. Above the stage was a gallery that, when it wasn't occupied by musicians or wealthy patrons, could suggest any kind of high place—castle ramparts, a cliff, or a balcony.

Special effects were common. A trap door in the main stage allowed ghosts to appear. Even more spectacularly, supernatural beings could be lowered from above the stage. For added realism, actors hid bags of pig's blood and guts under their stage doublets. When pierced with a sword, the bags spilled out over the stage and produced a gory effect.

All these staging methods and design elements greatly appealed to Elizabethan audiences and made plays increasingly popular. By the time Shakespeare died in 1616, there were more than 30 theaters in and around London.

What would Shakespeare, so accustomed to the rough-and-tumble stagecraft of the Globe, think of the theaters where his plays are performed today? He would probably miss some of the vitality of the Globe. For centuries now, his plays have been most often performed on stages with a frame called the "proscenium arch," which cleanly separates the audience from the performers. This barrier tends to cast a peculiar shroud of privacy over his plays so that his characters do not seem to quite enter our world.

But with greater and greater frequency, Shakespeare's plays are being performed out-of-doors or in theaters with three- or four-sided stages. And a replica of the Globe Theatre itself opened in London in 1996, only about 200 yards from the site of the original. This new Globe is an exciting laboratory where directors and actors can test ideas about Elizabethan staging. Their experiments may change our ideas about how Shakespeare's plays were performed and give new insights into their meaning.

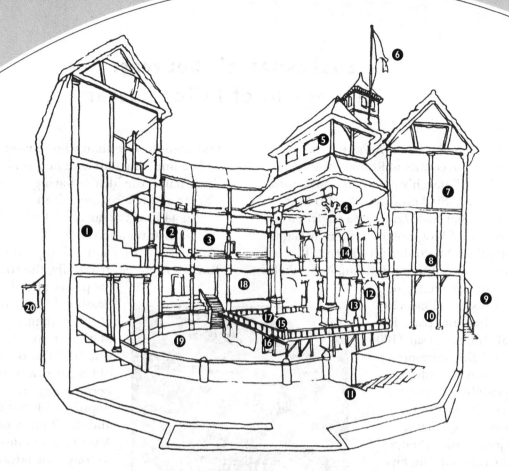

1 Corridor A passageway serving the middle gallery.

2 Entrance Point leading to the staircase and upper galleries.

3 Middle Gallery The seats here were higher priced.

4 The Heavens So identified by being painted with the zodiac signs.

5 Hut A storage area that also held a winch system for lowering characters to the stage.

6 Flag A white flag above the theatre meant a show that day.

7 Wardrobe A storage area for costumes and props.

8 Dressing Rooms Rooms where actors were "attired" and awaited their cues.

9 Tiring-House Door The rear entrance or "stage door" for actors or privileged spectators.

10 Tiring-House Backstage area providing space for storage and business.

11 Stairs Theatregoers reached the galleries by staircases enclosed by stairwells.

12 Stage Doors Doors opening into the Tiring-House.

13 Inner Stage A recessed playing area often curtained off except as needed.

14 Gallery Located above the stage to house musicians or spectators.

15 Trap Door Leading to the hell area where a winch elevator was located.

16 Hell The area under the stage, used for ghostly comings and goings or for storage.

17 Stage Major playing area jutting into the pit, creating a sense of intimacy.

18 Lords Rooms or private galleries. Six pennies let a viewer sit here, or sometimes on stage.

19 The Pit Sometimes referred to as "the yard," where the "groundlings" watched.

20 Main Entrance Here the doorkeeper collected admission.

Shakespeare's Sources:
The Legend of Julius Caesar

Shakespeare based *Julius Caesar* on written accounts of Roman history, especially Plutarch's *Lives of the Noble Greeks and Romans.* Shakespeare may also have been familiar with *Lives of the Caesars,* a collection of biographies written by Gaius Tranquillus Suetonius (70–140 A.D.), a secretary to Emperor Hadrian. Nevertheless, Shakespeare changed many historical facts to fit his fictional play. The "real" Julius Caesar (100–44 B.C.) first became popular as the official responsible for putting on combats with wild beasts and gladiators. He joined with Pompey and Crassus in the First **triumvirate**—a form of government in which power is controlled by three people. As his fame as a brilliant military general grew, so did his own power.

Caesar defeated Pompey and his followers in the Battle of Pharsalus in 48 B.C. Caesar then returned to Rome. By 46 B.C., he had been named dictator for life.

Fears of his ambition grew with the arrival of Cleopatra in Rome. Caesar had met the queen of Egypt in 48 B.C. She and Caesar fell in love and had a child. The Romans knew that Cleopatra was a charming and ambitious woman who wanted Caesar to become king and take her as his queen. They hated the idea of having to bow before Caesar and his foreign queen.

In 44 B.C., Caesar was killed by his best friend, Brutus, and others. The assassins claimed that they wanted to preserve the Roman republic. Ironically, the struggle for power after Caesar's death led to the birth of the Roman Empire. Mark Antony (83–30 B.C.), who had also been one of Caesar's best friends, became a great general, popular with both the army and the Roman people. After Caesar's death, Antony took advantage of the chaos to ally himself with Caesar's heir, Octavius, and another general, Lepidus. With his allies, Antony defeated Brutus and Cassius at the Battle of Philippi. The Second triumvirate ruled ruthlessly, killing hundreds of political enemies. After a quarrel with Octavius, Antony joined forces with Cleopatra of Egypt. The two attempted to overthrow Octavius, but they were defeated at the Battle of Actium in 31 B.C. Antony and Cleopatra committed suicide, and Octavius became the sole ruler of Rome.

Cleopatra

Julius Caesar Timeline

509 B.C. Lucius Junius Brutus rebels against the brutal tyrant Tarquin the Proud and establishes the Roman republic.

202 B.C. Rome defeats Carthage in the Second Punic War and becomes a major military power.

100 B.C. Julius Caesar is born.

82 B.C. Lucius Cornelius Sulla becomes dictator of Rome. Sulla plans to have Caesar assassinated as part of a purge. Caesar flees Rome. Sulla later relents, and Caesar returns.

65 B.C. Caesar gains popularity as *aedile*, or director of public works and games, by putting on combats with wild beasts and gladiators.

63 B.C. Caesar is elected *pontifex maximus*, head of the state religion.

60 B.C. The First triumvirate (Caesar, Pompey, and Crassus) rules Rome.

59 B.C. Caesar is elected consul, one of Rome's two executive officers, in a fixed election. He marries Calphurnia. Julia, Caesar's daughter by his first marriage, weds Pompey.

55 B.C. Caesar invades Germany and leads military expeditions to Britain.

54 B.C. Julia dies, and tension grows between Caesar and Pompey; Caesar invades Britain again.

51 B.C. Caesar completes his conquest of Gaul.

49 B.C. Caesar refuses Pompey's order to give up his army and begins civil war. He appoints himself tribune for life and dictator.

48 B.C. Caesar falls in love with Cleopatra and defeats Pompey's army at Pharsalus. (He pardons Brutus and Cassius, who fought against him, and appoints them to high office.)

45 B.C. Caesar becomes the only ruler of the Roman republic.

44 B.C. Caesar is named dictator for life (February);

Caesar refuses crown offered by Mark Antony (March);

Caesar plans to lead an army to avenge the defeat of Crassus (March);

Caesar is assassinated (March);

Antony forms the Second triumvirate with Octavius and Lepidus.

43 B.C. Cicero is among the 300 senators and 2,000 businessmen who die by order of the Second triumvirate.

42 B.C. Brutus and Cassius commit suicide after Antony defeats them at Philippi.

41 B.C. Antony joins forces with Cleopatra; they plan to rule the new Roman Empire.

31 B.C. Octavius defeats Antony at Actium; Antony and Cleopatra commit suicide, and Octavius becomes sole ruler of Rome.

27 B.C. Octavius becomes the first Roman Emperor

Caesar

Notes

Notes

Notes

Notes

Notes